Albert Ellis

Rational Emotive Behavior Therapy

Publisher's Note

This publication is designed to provide accurate and authoritative information in regard to the subject matter covered. It is sold with the understanding that the publisher is not engaged in rendering psychological, medical, or other professional service.

Books in The Practical Therapist Series® *present authoritative answers to the question, "What-do-I-do-now-and-how-do-I-do-it?" in the practice of psychotherapy, bringing the wisdom and experience of expert mentors to the practicing therapist. A book, however, is no substitute for thorough professional training and adherence to ethical and legal standards. At minimum:*

- *The practitioner must be qualified to practice psychotherapy.*

- *Clients participate in psychotherapy only with informed consent.*

- *The practitioner must not "guarantee" a specific outcome.*

— Robert E. Alberti, Ph.D., Publisher

Other Titles in The Practical Therapist Series®

Creative Therapy with Children and Adolescents

Integrative Brief Therapy

Meditative Therapy

Metaphor in Psychotherapy

Rational
Emotive
Behavior
Therapy

A Therapist's
Guide

Albert Ellis, Ph.D.
Catharine MacLaren, M.S.W.

The Practical Therapist Series®

Impact 🕮 Publishers®
ATASCADERO, CALIFORNIA

Impact Publishers and colophon are registered trademarks of Impact Publishers, Inc.

ATTENTION ORGANIZATIONS AND CORPORATIONS:
This book is available at quantity discounts on bulk purchases for educational, business, or sales promotional use. For further information, please contact Impact Publishers, P.O. Box 6016, Atascadero, CA 93423-6016 (Phone: 1-800-246-7228).

Library of Congress Cataloging-in-Publication Data

Ellis, Albert.
    Rational emotive behavior therapy : a therapist's guide / Albert Ellis and Catharine MacLaren.
      p.   cm. -- (The practical therapist series)
    Includes bibliographical references and index.
    ISBN 1--886230-12-9 (alk. paper)
    1. Rational-emotive psychotherapy.   I. MacLaren, Catharine.
    II. Title.   III. Series.
    RC489.R3E464   1998
    616.89'14--DC21   98.7505
                                                       CIP

Cover design by Sharon Schnare, San Luis Obispo, California
Printed in the United States of America on acid-free paper
Published by **Impact ✿ Publishers®**
POST OFFICE BOX 6016
ATASCADERO, CALIFORNIA 93423-6016
www.impactpublishers.com

Dedication

Dedicated to Janet L. Wolfe
—— Albert Ellis

Dedicated to Elizabeth M. Love-Brockway and my parents
—— Catharine MacLaren

Contents

Introduction

O ur primary goal with *Rational Emotive Behavior Therapy: A Therapist's Guide* is to present you, the mental health professional, with a comprehensive look at Rational Emotive Behavior Therapy (REBT) in an easy-to-read format.

The first portion of the book focuses on answering the questions: How, when, and where did REBT originate? We discuss the philosophically based origins of the theory as well as the core reasons that people become disturbed and stay disturbable.

We have then devoted several chapters to the actual hands-on practice of REBT. We begin with a discussion of the assessment phase of therapy and then describe the variety of specific cognitive, emotive, and behavioral interventions commonly used in this approach. We have also included numerous case examples in order to facilitate your learning process.

Finally, we have included a chapter on integrating REBT with a range of other theoretical frameworks. Whether you are a newcomer to the field or a seasoned professional, we hope that you enjoy this book and use it as a reference guide in the future.

1

Rational Emotive Behavior Theory: An Introduction and a Reflection

R ational Emotive Behavior Therapy is based on the assumption that cognition, emotion, and behavior are not disparate human functions but are, instead, intrinsically integrated and holistic. When we feel, we think and act; when we act, we feel and think; and when we think, we feel and act. Why? Because humans rarely, except for a few moments at a time, just feel, or just think, or just behave.

When people are disturbed, they think-feel-act in a dysfunctional, self-defeating manner and when they undisturb themselves they almost invariably change some of their cognitions, change their emotional reactions, *and* change their activities. Susan, one of AE's* clients, was panicked about talking to attractive men and therefore avoided them at dances, social, and other gatherings. She perceived them as "dangerous," felt severe anxiety when she encountered them, and bolted away from them when it looked like they might approach her. She *thought* them "dangerous," *felt* panic, and *acted* avoidantly.

After several sessions of REBT Susan mainly realized that she was telling herself that she *absolutely must not* be rejected by

---

*Throughout the book the authors are identified by their initials: "AE" = Albert Ellis; "CM" = Catharine MacLaren.

attractive men or else *she* was a reject and a *worthless person*. She changed her core Irrational Beliefs to, "I *prefer* to avoid rejection by attractive men but if I am rejected that merely proves that I failed this time, can learn from my rejection, and can perhaps do better next time. But even if I always fail with them, I'm merely frustrated and handicapped in one important area of my life and can enjoy relationships with less attractive men."

As noted in the theory of REBT, Susan changed one of her core negative cognitions, and thereby helped herself reduce her panic and avoidance. That sounds good, and supposedly "proves" that her changing her Irrational Beliefs made Susan less anxious and phobic. Actually, Susan changed her core Beliefs, all right, but she also, whether she realized it or not, changed several other perceptions and cognitions, such as: 1) Attractive men are "dangerous." 2) Rejection by them is "horrible." 3) "Unless one really favors me, I can't be happy at all." 4) "Every time I risk it and fail with one, that makes me a totally worthless individual." 5) "If I settle for a less attractive man, people will see I weakly gave in and will consider me a loser."

So Susan's main cognitions were complex and led to other negative cognitions — which, in turn, tended to change when she changed one or two of her Irrational Beliefs. Moreover, Susan's feelings changed from panic to concern — a healthy negative feeling that allowed her thereafter to converse with attractive men and only feel sorry and disappointed if they rejected her. With her new Rational Beliefs, she *felt* comfortable on seeing attractive men approach her, at times she actually *felt* happy to see them approach, she *felt* like staying and talking to them, she *felt* interested and absorbed when she conversed with them, and she had various related feelings.

As for her actions, when she stopped believing that she *absolutely must not* be rejected by attractive men, and that she *was* a *worthless person* if they rejected her, she soon took several actions along with stopping her phobia about them. 1) She looked, often, for attractive men, instead of looking away from them. 2) She actually *approached* some of them herself. 3) She *arranged* for some introductions to them. 4) She *talked animatedly* to them. 5) She tried to get some of them to date her. Et cetera.

'Moral: According to REBT, disturbed and less disturbed thoughts, feelings, and actions are complicated, varied, and significantly affect each other. The REBT perspective remains as AE described it over forty years ago:

> Instead, then, of saying, "Jones thinks about this puzzle," we should more accurately say, "Jones perceives-moves-feels-thinks about this puzzle." Because, however, Jones' activity in reaction to the puzzle may be *largely* focused upon solving it and only *incidentally* on seeing, manipulating, and feeling about it, we may perhaps justifiably emphasize only his thinking. Emotion is not one thing but a combination and holistic integration of several seemingly diverse, yet actually closely related, phenomena (Ellis, 1958, p. 35).

❖ *Integrative and Eclectic Aspects of REBT*

In REBT's therapeutic endeavor to help people change their Irrational Beliefs to Rational Beliefs and thus improve their emotional and behavioral functions, it is always integrative. REBT uses many multimodal methods (Lazarus 1989) — cognitive, emotive, and behavioral. But it integrates them and helps clients to see how they importantly affect each other.

REBT has a number of unique theories, as we shall show in later chapters, it bases its practice on its theory, and is not merely "eclectic." Its theory also incorporates significant parts of other therapeutic systems. Thus, it reveals clients' *unconscious motives and defense systems,* as Freudians do. It uses Jung's concept of *self-actualization.* It includes Rogers' theory and practice of *unconditional positive regard* or full acceptance. It energetically *encourages clients to change,* as Adlerians do. It actively-directively gives *homework assignments,* uses *operant conditioning,* and employs *in vivo desensitization* as Skinnerians and other behaviorists do. It uses many *experiential, encounter, and feeling methods,* as Gestalt therapists do. At times, though rarely, it even uses *irrational and magical* techniques, when clients are "allergic" to rational ones.

REBT integrates some aspects of many therapeutic theories, and eclectically uses specific techniques from many sources for individual clients who may not follow its favorite methods. Further discussion of integrating REBT with other approaches can be found in chapter 8.

The Effectiveness of REBT

AE originated REBT because it was more effective than other forms of therapy. In the first major article on it (Ellis, 1958, p. 49), he predicted "psychotherapy which includes a high dosage of rational analysis... will prove to be more effective with more types of clients than any of the non-rational or semi-rational therapies now being widely employed." Forty years of research on psychotherapy has shown that prediction to be partly substantiated by hundreds of studies of REBT and CBT. But only partly!

First of all, AE's theory that people have both Rational Beliefs (RBs) and Irrational Beliefs (IBs) and that when they have frequent and intense IBs they tend to be more disturbed than when they hold fewer and weaker IBs, has been backed by considerable evidence. Well over a thousand published studies have backed this hypothesis (Clark, 1997; Glass & Arnkoff, 1997; Schwartz, 1997). According to these studies, people's acknowledged IBs and their degree of emotional disturbance seem to be significantly correlated. Thus, one of the major hypotheses of REBT has much evidence to back it.

AE's second major theory — that when people change their IB's to more Rational Beliefs, either in therapy or by self-help procedures, they become significantly less disturbed — also has a great deal of confirming evidence behind it. Over 250 controlled studies of the effectiveness of REBT have been published, and the great majority of them show positive results (McGovern & Silverman, 1984; Lyons & Woods, 1991; Silverman, McCarthy & McGovern, 1991). More than a thousand studies have been published on the efficacy of various kinds of cognitive behavioral therapy (CBT), and again the great majority of them show it to be effective (Dobson, 1989; Hollon & Beck, 1994). No other form of psychotherapy except behavior therapy has produced such good experimental results, and today behavior therapy usually includes many cognitive methods.

REBT and CBT, as can be seen, have excellent experimental findings and have been shown to be widely effective with a large variety of clients. More and more aspects of them are now being "snuck in" to many other therapy systems!

❖ The Origins of REBT

The origin of rational emotive behavior therapy goes back to 1953, when AE abandoned psychoanalysis.

> I had practiced analysis for six years, but I found it to be quite inefficient. At best, I helped my clients to see some of the psychodynamic aspects of their disturbances, but not how to change their thinking, their emoting, and their behaving so they could undo the self-defeating aspects of their lives. Presumably, they understood how

they got the ways they were ---- but not what to do to change.

Thus, one client gained insight into the fact that he unconsciously hated his father and that he had "transferred" that feeling into hating his boss and other males who had traits similar to his parent; but he was not at all successful at giving up his self-sabotaging actions toward his wealthy and dominating father nor his powerful and dictatorial boss. His dramatic "insight" into his problems with strong men and his gush of feelings when this occurred helped him very little.

This and several other cases, where insight and expression of repressed feelings just didn't work, "set me to do some tall thinking about psychotherapy."

First, I went back to my prepsychoanalytic techniques of therapy, particularly those I had learned in sex and marital therapy, and started giving my clients activity homework assignments and skill training. That worked much better, particularly with socially phobic clients, who had considerable insight into the supposed origins of their inhibitions but who still refused to use this insight to relate to others. Within a few weeks of *in vivo* desensitization and relationship training, they made more progress than they had in a year or more of psychoanalysis. Interesting! So I kept slipping behavioral methods into my analytic therapy.

Even more valuable to my therapeutic approach was my revision of the whole concept of insight. I began to see that giving clients insight into the past helped a few clients see that, however badly they were treated as children, they still did not have to react in the same immature way today. So they forgave their parents and went on with their lives. But the great majority who had the same dramatic insights hardly improved at all. They still hated their parents and themselves. No, the more traditional concept of insight is not enough for deep and lasting personal change. The reality is that most of us are very good at identifying the wrongs which we have experienced during our lifetimes but that knowledge, in and of itself, rarely produces lasting and positive change. In fact, without appropriate steps to reconcile and move on from those negative experiences, it can often result in extremely unhelpful self-pity and have a "retraumatizing" effect on some individuals.

I thought about this, and realized that the *kind* of insight that clients usually gain in most forms of therapy isn't very helpful. It doesn't show them what they are *now* doing to keep alive the hurts and horrors of the past — or, for that matter, what they did *then,* during their childhood, to make themselves hurt and horrified. Why did they get so upset in the first place? What were they now doing to retain, or even worsen, this upsetness? What about insight into *that?*

I had always been interested in philosophy, especially the philosophy of human happiness, and made it one of my own hobbies from the age of sixteen onward. So I re-read many of the ancient and modern philosophers to help me come up with answers to these important questions. Fortunately, they did help. For many philosophers — especially the ancient Asians, Gautama Buddha and Lao-Tsu and the ancient Greeks and Romans Epicurus, Epictetus, and Marcus Aurelius — had clearly seen what the psychoanalysts and the behaviorists neglected: that humans are constructivists who don't merely get disturbed by external influences but also significantly contribute to and maintain their own dysfunctional thinking, feelings, and doings. As Epictetus nicely put it two thousand years ago, "People are disturbed not by things but by the views they take of them!" Phenomenalism, constructivism, and postmodernism! I am happy to say that in the 1950's I managed to bring Epictetus out of near-obscurity and make him famous all over again.

❖ The History of REBT

Sparked by philosophy, I worked on my psychothera-peutic theory from 1953 to 1955, and finally came up with what I first called Rational Therapy (RT) in January 1955 (Ellis 1957a, 1957b, 1958). In it, I presented the rather unique ABC theory of emotional disturbance. This held that when people were confronted with Adversity (A) and reacted with disturbed Consequences (C), such as severe anxiety and depression, it was largely their Belief System (B), together with A, that led to their dysfunctions. Thus, A x B=C. This theory significantly differed from psychoanalytic, conditioning, and other popular theories of emotional disturbance that were popular in 1955.

Now cognitive conceptions of psychotherapy were not entirely new, and were espoused by Pierre Janet (1898), Paul Dubois (1902), Alfred Adler (1929), and other therapists in the early twentieth century. But in the 1950's they were quite unpopular, having been overwhelmed by psychodynamic and, to a lesser degree, conditioning ideas. So when I heavily emphasized B (Beliefs) in the ABC's of Rational Therapy, I at first had few followers. Using my own Belief System to bolster me, however — and particularly convincing myself that I didn't *have* to have the approval of other therapists, though it would be nice to have it — I persisted in promulgating REBT as a pioneering form of cognitive-behavioral therapy (CBT) in spite of almost universal opposition. I wrote and lectured extensively on the subject until, in the 1960's, several capable practitioners followed me with their own versions of CBT — including Glasser (1965), Beck (1976), Bandura (1997), and Meichenbaum (1977).

My innovations in therapy not only put a high premium on the use of cognition but also for the first time welded it with behavior therapy, so that RT became the first of the major cognitive behavior therapies. This was because I used some of the behavioral techniques of John B. Watson (Watson, 1919) to conquer my own public speaking phobia and my own social anxiety when I was 19 years old. Also, before I became a psychoanalyst, I used behavioral methods in sex therapy and general psychotherapy. When I stopped calling myself a psychoanalyst in 1953, I started using these behavioral methods more, and I incorporated them into Rational Therapy when I began to do it in 1955 and became a pioneering cognitive behavior therapist.

As I said in my first major paper on it, at the American Psychological Association Convention in Chicago on August 31, 1956, Rational Therapy was also highly active-directive, confrontational, and emotive. But, because of its title, therapists often failed to acknowledge its emotional aspects. In 1961, I and Robert Harper, who was my leading collaborator, changed its name to Rational-Emotive Therapy (RET). Raymond Corsini rightly objected to this designation for over twenty years, as he said that RET had a very strong behavioral aspect and therefore should preferably be called Rational Emotive Behavior Therapy.

I wrongly argued with Ray, because RET became very popular in the 1960's, but I finally admitted that he was right and I was wrong. So in 1993 I formally changed the name to Rational Emotive Behavior Therapy (Ellis, 1993), which I think will be its final designation. It describes, in a fairly precise manner, the kind of comprehensive, integrative, and multimodal system that it actually is.

2

The Philosophic and Personality Theory Foundations of REBT

R EBT has, at its foundation, two kinds of theories. First, its philosophical outlook and its general theory of human personality and its disturbance. Second, its theories of therapeutic change. These sets of theories integrate with each other in some important respects. In this chapter we will mainly consider REBT's philosophic outlook and the questions of personality and why some people seem to be more disturbed than are others.

❖ Postmodern Philosophy and REBT

AE originated REBT as a logical positivist — one who believed that truth was not absolute or pure but that as scientists we come close to it by finding the facts of a situation and then drawing conclusions from these facts. Truth was indeed only temporary because, as Karl Popper (1985) showed, even when a hypothesis is backed up by a good deal of evidence later factual discoveries may falsify it.

Logical positivism has its limitations, as has been shown by Popper (1985), Bartley (1984), and Mahoney (1991), and has been especially shown to be shaky by several postmodernist thinkers (Derrida, 1976; Feyerband, 1975; Gergen, 1995). They point out that "facts" and "truths" are always identified by people and therefore seem to have no "objective" or "true" reality. For many years something of a phenomenologist and existentialist, AE has also become a moderate, not a radical, postmodernist. REBT always was fairly postmodern, because it is notably against absolute musts and shoulds, and therefore opposed to the notion of absolute truth. Its main postmodern ideas are these, as outlined in, "Postmodern ethics for active-directive counseling and psychotherapy" (Ellis, 1997).

1) Perhaps some kind of indubitable objective reality or thing in itself exists, but we only seem to know it through our fallible, personal-social, different and changing human perceptions. We do not have any absolute certainty about what reality is or what it will be — despite our being often strongly convinced that we do.

2) Our views of what is good or bad, what is right and wrong, what is moral and immoral are, as George Kelly (1955) pointed out, largely personal-social *constructions*. The identification of universal truths is an impossible task and all ethical beliefs have a constructive nature.

3) Although human personality has some important innate and fairly fixed elements, it also largely arises from relational and social influences and is much less individualistic than is commonly thought.

4) People are importantly influenced or conditioned by their cultural rearing. Their behaviors are amazingly multicultural and there is no conclusive evidence that their diverse cultures are right or wrong, better or

worse than others (Ivey & Ragazio-DiGilio, 1991; Sampson, 1990).

Either/or concepts of goodness and badness often exist and are rigidly held, but they tend to be inaccurate, limited, and prejudiced. More open-minded perceptions of humans tend to show that things and processes exist on a *both/and* and an *and/also* basis. Because monolithic, either/or, all/none solutions to problems have their limitations, we had better consider a range of alternate, and/also solutions and test them out to see how well — and how badly — they work.

5) Just about all solutions we strive to achieve for our problems depend on choosing our goals and purposes from which to work. These are always arguable, never absolute. We can arrive at a consensus as to what goals and purposes to choose but not at any absolute agreement as to which are better and worse.

REBT has sometimes been seen as nonconstructionist (Guidano, 1991; Mahoney, 1991), but it actually is unusually constructionist. It emphasizes people thinking and working in a flexible and adaptive manner. It holds that rigid, absolutistic *musts* by which people often upset themselves are learned from their culture but are also created by their own creative and biological tendencies. It helps clients to see how they create core dysfunctional philosophies and how they can constructively change them by thinking, by thinking about their thinking, and by thinking about thinking about their thinking (Dryden, 1995; Ellis, 1994, 1996; Ellis & Dryden, 1975; Ellis, Gordon, Neenan, & Palmer, 1998). In dealing with problems of self-worth it agrees with the constructionist and existentialist position of Heidegger (1962), Tillich (1953), and Rogers (1961) that humans can define themselves as worthy just because they choose to do so. It deals with unconscious and tacit processes that create disturbance and abet problem solving. It holds that people have considerable natural ability to reconstruct and change themselves but it actively-directively tries to help them to do so in collaboration with an involved therapist. It emphasizes the use of the flexible, nondogmatic method of scientific hypothesizing and checking on hypotheses and the empirical exploration of values and standards to see what results they tend to produce.

❖ *Philosophical Emphasis of REBT*

As noted above, much of the theory of REBT was derived from philosophy rather than psychology. As also noted, REBT is cognitive, emotive, and behavioral, and is not by any means strictly "intellectual." But in some ways it favors clients making profound philosophical changes instead of only disputing their specific Irrational Beliefs and automatic negative thoughts and coming up with more sensible ones. Nor does it favor what is called "positive thinking," or the replacing of negative thoughts with optimistic ones that sometimes are pollyannaish.

Donald, for example, irrationally believed that he was a bad person because he had cheated his brother, David, out of part of the money their mother had left them in her will. Donald was executor of the will and illegitimately deducted several extra thousands of dollars for expenses in settling the estate and David naively accepted this. So Donald considered himself, a year later, a "rotten thief," and was ashamed to tell David what he had done. He beat himself mercilessly and got depressed.

Donald saw a hypnotist for several sessions who used positive thinking to help Donald see that he had done many good things, including helping David, for most of his life, but only a few bad things, such as cheating David. His positive thinking mantra, which he was to repeat strongly to himself many times, was, "I do many more good than bad deeds, therefore I am a basically good person."

This positive thinking worked for a while, but then Donald soon got very guilty and depressed again, and became quite disillusioned with the efficacy of his positive thought. When he came to see AE for REBT, he still held the covered up Irrational Belief, "I *absolutely must* not do any distinctly bad deeds. The good acts I do hardly erase the bad ones, which are never permissible. A *really* bad act, such as I did when cheating David, makes me a rotten person! I therefore deserve to suffer and be depressed. Only enough suffering will make me a good person. I'm really rotten to the core!"

Donald's positive thinking only shunted aside his demand that he never do bad deeds and for awhile covered up his negative, self-downing thinking — but it did not remove it. With REBT, AE helped him actively dispute his Irrational Beliefs and truly give them up. As a result of his doing so, together with doing some REBT "shame-attacking exercises" (explained on page 94) and forcing himself to honestly tell David what he had done, Donald began to see and work at adopting several core philosophies: 1) "There is no reason why I *absolutely must not* do any real bad deeds, though it is *highly preferable* that I not do them." 2) "I will always be a fallible human who, alas, will sometimes act poorly. Too bad, but I will do my best to behave *less* fallibly, rather than *in*fallibly." 3) "Doing a bad *act* cannot make me, globally, a *bad person,* only a *person who* does some evil things, and had better try to correct them."

When, by strongly disputing and acting against his Irrational Beliefs, and thereby arriving at some core Rational Beliefs, (what REBT calls profound Effective New Philosophies), Donald truly undermined (not covered up) his disturbed thinking-feeling-behaving. He was then able to become less depressed and less depress*ive*. He *got* better rather than, with the positive thinking, merely *felt* better (which we explain in more detail in the next section). So we strive, in using REBT, to help people make a profound philosophical change — fundamentally changing their outlook and keeping it changed. This seems to go beyond changing their automatic negative thoughts to changing their *core Irrational Beliefs*. Doing so is a deeper form of thinking that we shall turn to again.

❖ *Multicultural Aspects of REBT*

REBT is unusually open to clients who come from different cultures and from minority groups within the same culture. This is largely because its central theory opposes absolutistic, rigid thinking but encourages individuals and groups to have innumerable preferences, goals, desires, and standards — as long as they do not dogmatically and dictatorially insist that they and others absolutely must follow them. If clients have inclinations that are significantly different from the standards of their family, culture, religious, or political group, but they do not break the law or harm others with these standards, REBT rarely discourages them. REBT clearly points out, however, that when they hold their goals and values in self-dictatorial or other-dictatorial ways, they will often get into individual and social trouble. Therefore, it would usually be best if they kept their personal and cultural rules, but held them as strong preferences instead of grandiose musts or commands.

Therapists who use REBT theories and practices are therefore free to help different clients to achieve their own goals and values but to refrain from taking them to "musturbatory" extremes. Extremism and rigidity will often sabotage their personal and social purposes. Flexible, but still definite, standards usually will not. REBT practitioners therefore are able to fully accept — not blamefully condemn — clients from widely differing backgrounds, cultures, and religious orientations.

❖ *How Does REBT Define Rational and Irrational?*

To some people, *rational* is a "bad word." It means many things to different people — some of which are not very rational!

As used in REBT, rational does *not* mean unemotional. Occasionally, we hear from clients who are new to REBT: "It seems as if you don't want me to feel anything. Do you want me to go through life as an unemotional zombie?" *Not at all!* Rational people often had better be highly emotional — such as distinctly sorry, disappointed, and annoyed when things go wrong in their lives. As Windy Dryden has said, rational when used in REBT means "that which helps people to achieve their basic goals and purposes, whereas 'irrational' means that which prevents them from achieving these goals and purposes" (Dryden, 1984, p. 238). Otherwise put, rational means self-helping and irrational means self-defeating.

However, because your clients choose to live in a social group, rational also means helping the group to survive and to achieve its basic goals, and irrational means seriously interfering with the group's survival and well-being. Also, to be rational usually means being efficient in achieving one's individual and community goals, but efficiency and rationality are not the same: since one can efficiently bring about self-defeating and social-defeating ends.

Rational, again, is a word that has many meanings, some of them contradictory. From your clients' view it normally means self-helping — getting more of what they want and less of what they don't want. It is largely individualistic. But clients can choose to put social interests above their self-interest—and to some degree, as Adler (1929) showed, that *is* mental health as well as community health. But even individualistic clients want to be accepted by others and are likely to be miserable when they are not. So individual mental adjustment overlaps with treating others nicely and properly. For both the individual's and society's sake it would seem rational to strike a balance between self-interest and social-interest — which is not easy!

As postmodernists and constructionists, we can have no absolute, essential view of rationality, just as we can have no "true" view of what is "good" or "moral." People can agree on "rational" goals, but hardly always do. Assuming that your clients wish to be less panicked, depressed, and enraged, you can help them to achieve this wish by using various REBT (and other therapeutic) methods. We therefore refer to these self-helping techniques as "rational." Most of the time they will work better than other methods. But that does not mean that under all conditions and at all times with all clients they are "rational" or "good." You can always be skeptical of their absoluteness and universality. Use them because you think they often or usually work. But remain open-minded and skeptical!

❖ *Healthy and Unhealthy Negative Feelings in REBT*

REBT has several theories regarding healthy and unhealthy negative feelings when clients are faced with Adversities in their lives. First, it holds that virtually all feelings are "natural" and almost automatically follow after thoughts of or actual experiences of stimuli that the client views as obnoxious or unpleasant. This in itself is a "healthy" human reaction, because if people did not have healthy negative feelings, they would not try to reduce or avoid negative stimuli and would live miserable lives and often fail to survive. Positive feelings also motivate people to survive and to be productive.

So REBT encourages people to feel, and often feel strongly, in positive and negative ways. It is not, as some therapists wrongly believe, "rational" in a sense of favoring lack of passion, stoicism, or unfeelingness. It is more Epicurean than Stoic.

REBT clearly distinguishes, however, when things go amiss, between *healthy* negative feelings — such as sorrow, regret, frustration, and annoyance — and *unhealthy* negative feelings — such as panic, depression, rage, and self-pity. Healthy negative feelings tend to produce self-helping and community-helping actions; unhealthy negative ones tend to interfere with reparative acts, or to result in inaction or destructive behavior. Thus, if one is concerned about failing a test, one studies harder to pass it. But if one is panicked about the possibility of failing it, one often avoids studying (which leads to more panic), studies anxiously and inefficiently, or doesn't take the test.

So REBT encourages your clients to feel strongly about succeeding at important tasks and relationships, but not to fall into the human propensity to raise their strong desires to absolutistic demands — "I *must* succeed or else I am worthless!" These produce dysfunctional negative feelings, especially panic and depression, that block their desires.

The REBT theories of *desires* and *preferences,* on the one hand, and *musts* and *demands* on the other hand, says that these personal tendencies are intrinsically related, and that virtually all humans have both of them. We all have — for innate, biological reasons as well as from family and cultural upbringing — varying strengths of desire — mild, moderate, and strong.

When people have strong desires, says REBT theory, they have (statistically) a greater tendency to make them into insistences and imperatives. Thus, your clients may *moderately* prefer that other people like them, and have little difficulty when some seem to dislike them. But if they *strongly* prefer approval, they are much more likely to insist, consciously and/or unconsciously, "People *must* like me! If some don't it's *awful* and shows that I am not a likeable person!"

Why people frequently turn their strong preferences and dislikes into internal commands is not entirely clear. Perhaps doing so helped them survive in primitive days when their social and physical environments were more dangerous.

❖ *Biology and Human Rationality and Irrationality*

REBT, unlike other psychotherapies that teach that human disturbance is primarily learned or conditioned, hypothesizes that people innately *and* by social teaching develop into rational *and* irrational thinkers. Obviously, they have to be largely rational and self-helping or they would not survive. They are born constructivists, so that when they face problems and any adversity that they consider against their best interests — especially that of not surviving — they are creative problem-solvers. That is their nature, from early childhood onward, just as it seems to be the nature of other living creatures, except more so. First, humans are more creative and inventive about what to think, feel, and do to survive. Second, they have a wider range of pleasurable activities — games, sports, art, music, science, etc. — that are not necessary for survival, though they seem to help. Third, they are more practical and self-actualizing than the other animals.

It is easy to emphasize human constructivism and to play down human destructivism. Defensively, we may not want to admit that we are often — damned often — irrational, self-defeating, socially immoral, and otherwise destructive of ourselves and others. As AE noted in a paper, "The Biological Basis of Human Irrationality" (Ellis, 1976), we cannot clearly prove that people are born, as well as reared, to be irrational, but there is a great deal of evidence to back this hypothesis. Witness:

1) Virtually all people sabotage themselves, and others, in many ways, despite their efforts and desires to do better.

2) Although cultural groups have widely different goals and values, their members easily add disturbance-creating irrationalities (absolute musts and demands) *about* their rules and standards. They thereby upset themselves.

3) Many human self-defeating behaviors exist — such as lack of discipline and procrastination — despite the self-helping teachings of people's parents, peers, and the mass media.

4) People who vigorously oppose "foolish" behaviors often engage in them. Agnostics exhibit absolutistic philosophies and highly religious individuals act immorally.

5) Millions of people acknowledge their self-harming behaviors, such as excessive drinking and drugging, yet consistently indulge in them.

6) Many individuals fall back to destructive acts, such as aggression and gambling, that they have worked hard to overcome.

7) People often find it easier to perform self-destructive acts, such as overeating, than to sensibly stop them.

8) Psychotherapists, who presumably know best what is destructive behavior, frequently engage in it.

So we see that virtually all people are born as well as raised to often be irrational, and that they easily disturb themselves. Fortunately, people are also largely rational; and they have a unique human quality of being able (through well developed language) to think about their irrational thinking, and to *think about thinking about* their thinking. So they are still constructivist.

You would do well to relieve many of your clients from self-damning by letting them know that, as humans will:

they often *easily* think, feel, and act defeatingly,

they *can* constructively change themselves, and

they require much work and practice to use their natural creativity to reduce their natural self-sabotaging.

3

The REBT Theory of Personality Disturbance and Change

REBT has several specific theories of how people become disturbed and what can be done to reduce or eliminate their disturbance. These theories overlap with other main theories of psychological disturbance but in some respects they are different. Here are some of their important differences.

❖ *Why and How People Become Psychologically Disturbed*

Psychological disturbance is varied and complicated and is by no means fully understood. It arises from people's biological tendencies to be constructivist (self-helping) and destructivist (self-defeating) and the interaction of these tendencies with environmental conditions and social learning. People become disturbed in many different ways and partly because of many different conditions. We may well discover some, but not all, of the main reasons for their disturbances. Especially in the case of a specific individual, we may again discover some of the main "causes," but not all the "causes," for her or his emotional and behavioral problems.

REBT hypothesizes that people are disturbed cognitively, emotionally, and behaviorally — yes, in all three ways — and that we had better designate them as being cognitively-emotionally-behaviorally self-defeating and other-defeating, because they *interactionally* make themselves upset. They may primarily (but not only) have thinking, emotional, or behavioral problems, but they also have aspects of the other two modes of disturbance. It is assumed that just about all humans are somewhat dysfunctional (for innate and social reasons) but have quite different degrees and kinds of dysfunction.

REBT especially emphasizes the cognitive elements in anxiety, depression and rage for several reasons:

- Disturbed cognitions (Irrational Beliefs) are often easily accessible, even when they are just below the surface of consciousness.

- Irrational Beliefs are frequently profound or core Beliefs that affect several important emotional and behavioral dysfunctions.

- Changing a core Irrational Belief, can sometimes effect a remarkable change in several dysfunctional feelings and behaviors, as the change generalizes to other areas. Changing only an emotion or a behavior may lead to more limited improvement.

- Making a profound philosophic change may reduce specific disturbances and also make the person less susceptible to future disturbances.

- Sometimes a cognitive change can be understood quickly, in a few sessions, while emotional and behavioral changes usually take more time, effort, and persistence.

For these and other reasons, REBT emphasizes philosophic methods, though it always uses several emotive and behavioral methods as well to facilitate and reinforce the changes. It encourages you as a therapist to experiment in the first few sessions with teaching your clients the ABC's of human disturbance, and how they can change B — their Belief System — and thereby often make some profound and lasting changes in C — their disturbed emotional and behavioral consequences.

Here is the main cognitive therapy theory of REBT — its ABC's. People, again, are easily distressed when they have goals and purposes (G) to stay alive and be happy and free from pain and when Adversity (A) interferes and they do not get what they want, or do get what they don't want. They have a choice of reacting to A with healthy negative feelings, such as sorrow, regret, and frustration, or reacting with unhealthy negative feelings, such as panic, depression, and rage. Largely, though not completely, they make this choice at B, their Belief System. When they choose rational or self-helping Beliefs, according to REBT, they often react with healthy feelings and actions; when they choose irrational or unhealthy Beliefs, they are more likely to react with unhealthy ones.

Keep in mind that many clients, at least at first, may not believe that they are mainly responsible for their reactions. The idea that they have choices about how they feel may be very foreign to them. Most of us are not socialized to take responsibility for our reactions. This is seen most clearly in some the language we use to describe situations. *"He made* me angry," *"It really* upset me," "She caused me to do it." These are all examples of the ways we attribute our emotions and behaviors to external sources. It may take a lot of work to show your client that, barring a mitigating biological condition, most times she becomes panicked, depressed, angry or otherwise irrationally upset, she's making a choice to do so. This, in turn, means that she has the power to choose a more flexible, realistic, and helpful reaction. This realization can be extremely empowering for clients.

People choose their Irrational or Rational Beliefs largely on the strength of their desires. When their strong desires for success, approval, and comfort are negated by Adversities they often irrationally demand that these A's *absolutely must* not exist. But when their desires are weak or moderate, they stick with rational preferences instead of musturbatory demands, and thereby less often disturb themselves when these preferences are not fulfilled.

People's evaluative Beliefs about Adversities are often automatic and unconscious; but they are also frequently conscious. What is largely unconscious is their knowledge that their Beliefs lead to (or at least significantly contribute to) their feelings. They usually have the illusion that they *just* feel bad about Adversity — that A "causes" C. Actually A x B=C. But since C frequently may occur almost instantly after A, they fail to see that B also importantly "causes" C. Particularly when A is very bad — say, they are falsely accused of theft — and they immediately feel enraged, they commonly think that the false accusation (A) by itself caused their rage (C), without realizing that their Beliefs (B) about A were also part of C.

The ABC theory of disturbance also says that when dysfunctional negative emotions occur, people have many different kinds of Irrational Beliefs (IBs) but they have several core IBs in addition to their having Rational Beliefs (RBs). The common core IBs that they hold include:

1) *Absolutistic musts and shoulds* — e.g., "I must not be falsely accused."

2) *Awfulizing* — e.g., it is awful and horrible to be falsely accused.

3) *I-can't-stand-it-itis* — e.g., "I can't stand being falsely accused." When people say "I can't stand it" they usually mean that the things they don't like are *so* bad that they *should not* exist. This is called low frustration tolerance or discomfort disturbance.

4)*Damning oneself and others* — e.g., "I am a *rotten person* if I am falsely accused and people think I really did steal." "My accusers are *bad people* for falsely accusing me."

REBT hypothesizes that people's core IBs interact with and influence each other. Thus, "I *must not* be falsely accused" often leads to the conclusion, "and it's *awful* when I am." But "It's *awful* for me to be falsely accused" often also leads to the conclusion, "Therefore I *must* not be!" The Beliefs that Adversities *absolutely must* not exist even when they indubitably do exist, is probably basic to awfulizing, I-can't-stand-it-itis, and damning of oneself and others, because if people only stayed with their preferences these seem to tacitly include a "but" that prevents the worst feelings of upsetness when they are not met.

Thus, "I *prefer* not to be falsely accused," implies "*but* if I am, it is *not* awful," "*but* if I am, I *can* stand it," and "*but* if I am, my accuser is not a wholly rotten person." So absolute *musts* and *must nots* seem to underlie other core IBs.

However, "I absolutely must not be falsely accused" implies that "Under all conditions and at all times I must never be falsely accused." It is therefore an arrant overgeneralization. Damning oneself and other people, as Korzybski (1933) pointed out, stems from the overgeneralized *is* of identity: "I *am* what I *do*. If my *act* is bad, I *am* bad." So along with musturbatory IBs we can look for basic overgeneralizations — evaluations of people and things that are illogical and unrealistic. Evaluating Adversities as *awful* implies that they are *totally* bad. Saying that we *can't stand* Adversities implies that we can't be happy *at all* with them. Designating John and Jill as *bad people* implies that they *only* and *always* act badly.

As far as your clients are concerned, you can show them that when they overgeneralize about Adversities in their lives, they can easily and profoundly disturb themselves. That will help them. But I have found that it is often simpler and easier for my clients to find their absolutistic musts and demands if they want to quickly see what they are doing — at B, their Belief System — to make their Adversities into emotional holocausts. An effective REBT maxim is "Cherchez le should! Cherchez le must!" "Find the should! Find the must!" This slogan will not tell your clients the whole or sole cause of their disturbances. But it will help them see the source that is one of the main accessible contributions to upsetness and that they have the ability to change.

Is the human Belief System involved in disturbances that are largely biological, such as endogenous depression and obsessive compulsive disorder (OCD), and those related to severe trauma, such as post-traumatic stress disorder? Very probably. In endogenous depression, neurotransmitters, particularly serotonin, work inefficiently to produce distorted perceptions and thoughts of a depressive nature; and in OCD several kinds of cognitive functions work poorly, such as fixed ideas, constant ruminations, and inability to do normal checking. Depression and OCD sufferers get depressed and anxious feelings, often without clear-cut causes, about which they then awfulize and damn themselves.

In PTSD the intensity, unexpectedness, and strangeness of traumas vastly shock people and lead to thoughts of severe rage, guilt, and self-deprecation. Also, the fear of the traumas reoccurring keeps the original feelings and panicked thoughts alive, sometimes for many years.

The REBT theory of disturbance can therefore explain much of the disturbance, and the disturbance about the disturbance, of many dysfunctions that have biological or severe environmental aspects.

REBT Theory of the Maintenance and Heightening of Emotional Disturbance

Once people become emotionally disturbed — for whatever reasons — their cognitions play a very important part in maintaining their dysfunctions. They remember Adversities, perceive that they could recur or worsen, and frequently demand a guarantee that they end. This keeps current "horrors" in mind and imagination augments and sustains them.

To make matters much worse, people often have Irrational Beliefs about their symptoms. Thus, Marcella had the IB that she *absolutely had to* do well in school, and whenever she experienced the Adversity of getting less than an A, she felt the Consequence (C) of depression. But then she made her depression into a real Adversity (A^2), told herself at IB^2, "I *must not* be depressed! It's *awful* to be depressed!" and wound up depressed about her depression (C^2).

Her condition went from bad to worse. Marcella saw AE for REBT, and at first agreed with its teachings but didn't improve. She then made failing at therapy into Adversity^3 and created IB^3 about her failure, especially, "I must do well at therapy! I'm no good for not working hard enough at it!" So she made herself depressed about her initial failure at therapy. In reverse order, AE helped her first accept herself while failing at therapy; second, accept herself in spite of her depression; and third, accept herself with a B or a C in a course. This triple-header unconditional self-acceptance (USA) challenged her core IBs about the *necessity* of doing well to be a worthwhile individual and helped her acquire several profound Rational Beliefs.

❖ The REBT Revealing of Irrational Beliefs

As noted previously in this book, several thinkers and therapists have come up with the idea that people largely disturb themselves with dysfunctional Beliefs. But which specific Beliefs they commonly used were not detailed and categorized until 1956, when AE first described twelve of them that were often used by clients when they were disturbed.

Then, after using REBT for a couple of years, AE realized that just about all the IBs clients held that helped make them and keep them disturbed could be placed under three major headings. Perhaps more importantly, each of these core dysfunctional Beliefs included an absolutistic must or demand. If, however, people held these same Beliefs as preferences or wishes, and rigorously refrained from escalating them into grandiose demands, they would minimize much (not all) of their disturbances. This, if valid, was a startling revelation; for it simplified the main cognitive factors in clients' upsetness, made them easily observable if therapists and clients looked for them, and presented workable solutions to changing them.

The three main musturbatory Irrational Beliefs that AE came up with were these:

1)"I *absolutely must* under all conditions do important
tasks well and be approved by significant others or else I
am an inadequate and unlovable person!" This Belief
often results in anxiety, depression, and feelings of
worthlessness or self-damnation when clients don't
function as well as they supposedly *must*. It includes the

illogical overgeneralizations of all-or-nothing thinking and labeling. Considering human fallibility, it is highly unrealistic.

2) "Other people *absolutely must* under all conditions treat me fairly and justly or else they are rotten, damnable persons!" This Irrational Belief often results in anger, rage, feuds, wars, genocide, and the denigration of others as a whole rather than mere judgement of their "bad" acts. Again it includes illogical overgeneralization and labeling and is unrealistic in the light of human fallibility.

3) "Conditions under which I live *absolutely must* always be the way I want them to be, give me almost immediate gratification, and not require me to work too hard to change or improve them; or else it is *awful,* I *can't stand* them, and it is impossible for me to be happy *at all!*" This IB results in low frustration tolerance or discomfort, disturbance, depression, procrastination, and inertia. It damns life or the world for being worse than it supposedly *should be.* Once again, it is illogical (for conditions, right now, are as "bad" as they are) and it is unrealistic (for ideal conditions rarely exist).

REBT doesn't oppose — in fact, it encourages — striving for success, approval, and comfort, as long as we *prefer* rather than *absolutely need* these things. Why? Because we are natural goal-seekers, enjoy striving, and usually (not always!) get better individual and social results. But when we (consciously or unconsciously) *demand* satisfactions, and well may *not* achieve them, watch it! Unhealthy misery, rather than healthy disappointment, frequently ensues — along with all kinds of unnecessary interferences.

In teaching your clients how to discover their dysfunctional, self-blocking Beliefs, should you try to help them uncover the specific IBs that encourage them, say, to feel depressed? Yes, by all means, as that will usually help them go on to D in the ABC's of REBT — *Disputing* their specific IB (which we discuss in chapter 5). But if they are depressed, consider first looking for all three of the major IBs to see if they can be found.

First, consider IB No. 1, "I *must* do well and gain approval!" A likely suspect when your clients feel depressed, as it often leads to self-downing. Are they really *insisting* that they do well in important tasks and/or be approved of by significant others? Get them to ask those questions as you, considering their goals and values, also do so.

Second, are your clients demanding that other people treat them well, and making themselves angry and depressed if these others are not acting the way they supposedly *must*? A real possibility — both of you had better explore it.

Third, are your depressed clients commanding that conditions *must* be good and *have to* give them what they want when they want it? Are they depressing themselves, with their low frustration tolerance, when conditions are not as good as they *absolutely should* be? Probably. But don't assume that they have this unrealistic IB — look for fairly clear evidence of it, and help them look, too.

The great value of REBT's hypothesizing three major Irrational Beliefs that often lead to disturbance is that you can fairly quickly, when the client presents a distinct emotional or behavioral problem, check to see if he or she holds one or more of the three and see if it is connected with this problem. Don't assume that it is connected — only assume that it *may* be held and that it *may* be connected. Often, and in a time-saving manner, you will be accurate.

Once you and the client discover a core IB, you can look for its subheadings and variations. For example a depressed client's Belief, "I *absolutely must* do well and be approved by significant others," may lead to other core derivative IBs. Such as:

- *Awfulizing:* "It's *awful* when John criticizes me!"

- *I-can't-stand-it-itis:* "I *can't stand* Mary's rejection!"

- *Overgeneralizing:* "If John and Mary criticize me, everyone also will, and I'll be totally alone!"

- *Jumping to conclusions:* "If John and Mary criticize me, I must be acting badly!"

- *Focusing on the negative:* "Mary is frowning, so she must be frowning at me."

- *Disqualifying the positive:* "John wants to go out with me but that's only because he has pity on me for being so inadequate."

- *Minimizing the good things:* "I spoke well in my conversation with John today, but I usually talk badly and he has a generally bad impression of me."

- *Personalizing:* "Mary says she's too busy to see anyone but she really means she doesn't want to see me."

- *Phoneyism:* "I went out of my way to be nice to John this time, but I'm really a phoney and far from a nice person."

- *Perfectionism:* "I got along nicely this time with John and Mary, but I made some stupid errors which I wouldn't have made if I were a perfectly adequate person. As I should be!"

If you and your clients turn up any important Irrational Beliefs that are leading to the feelings of depression, highlight them, show how they are connected with their depression, and show why they are unrealistic, illogical, and harmful. But at the same time reveal how they are involved with core IBs that they usually make pervasive and important.

The more you can help clients to reveal and surrender their core IBs, the more they can understand how to zero in on them, as well as to uncover their more specific and more limited IBs.

Helping Clients See the Connection Between their Beliefs, Feelings, and Actions
❖ ▬▬▬▬▬▬▬▬▬▬▬▬▬▬▬▬▬▬▬▬▬▬▬▬▬▬▬▬▬▬

One of the most important and self-sabotaging Irrational Beliefs held by disturbed clients is that, following Adversity (A) they automatically *just* have feeling and behavioral Consequences (C). Typical self-statements: "Closed spaces make me anxious." "You made me angry by treating me unfairly." "I felt like a worm when they laughed at me."

These are *partially* accurate statements of A (Adversity) and C (disturbed) feelings. But they omit the very important "B" factors — your clients' Beliefs about A. A alone clearly doesn't lead to C, for if it did all people in closed spaces would feel anxious, all would feel angry when they see others treating them unfairly, and all would feel like worms when they were laughed at. Obviously, and frequently, they all don't.

Helping your clients discover their IBs when they feel seriously disturbed may not be enough. Jonathan saw and "knew" he was often thinking irrationally when he concluded that his friends disliked him for beating them at tennis, even though they congratulated him and acted nicely to him after the game. Most of the evidence showed that they disliked losing the match but still liked him. Nevertheless, he still was angry at them for wanting to play with others, with whom they could succeed, rather than with him. He blamed his anger on the Adversity of their refusing to play with him. He at first didn't see what he was telling himself at B, namely, "They *shouldn't* avoid playing with me even if they lose. They'll play a more interesting and better game. They *should* really like me in spite of my winning and they don't like me well enough! Those lousy bastards!"

So Jonathan "saw" that his friends disliked him after he won a match, also "saw" that he exaggerated their dislike, but didn't see that his anger (C) stemmed not just from their refusal to play with him (A) but also from his *Beliefs* (B) about their refusal. When AE helped him to recognize B and its important contribution to C, he accepted the unpleasant fact of his friends' refusal to play. He made their playing with him a *preference* instead of a *demand* and felt sorry and disappointed about their refusal rather than angry at them.

Unless clients do see the BC connection, and realize that they can quickly find and change B, they will fail to learn and use one of the most important insights of REBT — and probably of therapy in general (Ellis & Dryden, 1997; Ellis & Harper, 1998; Walen, DiGiuseppe, & Dryden, 1992).

❖ The Use of Insight in REBT

Because it stresses cognition more than do some other therapies, REBT naturally emphasizes the importance of insight — of your clients recognizing what internal and external influences contributed to their disturbances and seeing what they can do to use them to improve their emotional and physical health. However, as noted above, REBT holds that insight itself may only partially help, and that understanding of the details of the *past* may interfere with understanding and changing *present* sources of dysfunction. REBT therefore emphasizes three main kinds of insight that are likely to help clients in the present.

Insight No. 1: (the ABC's of human disturbance): A (Adversity) often contributes significantly to C (Consequences) of disturbed feelings and behaviors, but so does B (Beliefs about A). A x B=C.

Insight No. 2: Even though disturbed C's frequently originated following Adversities (A's) in childhood and adolescence, they *then* were partially created by grandiose (though natural) IBs; and it is largely the *continued* Belief in these IBs that *keeps* the clients disturbed today. So they had better see these present and past IBs and change them to get better consequences today.

Insight No. 3: To improve clients' dysfunctional Consequences today usually requires a good deal of insight and *work and practice* — cognitive, emotive, and behavioral work and practice — because they have biological, learned, and habituated tendencies to maintain them (Ellis, 1994, 1996).

❖ *Getting Better Rather than Just Feeling Better*

"Helping people get better rather than merely feel better" (Ellis, 1972) is one of the key factors in REBT. The following points illustrate how that process works:

1) Clients come to see you, their therapist, to relieve their presenting symptoms — such as disturbed

emotions (e.g., severe anxiety, depression, rage, self-downing, and self-pity) and to stop their harmful compulsive reactions (e.g., violence, child abuse, over drinking, substance abuse, gambling, smoking, and overeating) and their withdrawal reactions (e.g., social phobias, public speaking phobias, and procrastination). Fine. First, help them minimize these self-defeating and socially harmful feelings and behaviors and preferably stop them in their tracks.

2) Clients, when they reduce the symptoms that bother them most, can be helped to minimize related or not-so-related thoughts, feelings, and behaviors. Thus, if they reduce their social anxiety, you can somewhat similarly show them how to reduce their work, their educational, their hypochondriacal, their phobic, and their other anxieties, which they may at first ignore or even be little aware of. Using the principles of REBT, they can be helped to minimize almost any kinds of anxiety, depression, and rage.

3) To get better, and not merely feel better, you can help them to rarely be anxious, depressed, or enraged about people and events that they have often upset themselves about previously. Their profound New Effective Philosophies become habitual and they rarely revert again to their former core Irrational Beliefs.

4) When they do upset themselves again, they can fairly easily reuse the various effective cognitive, emotive, and behavioral methods that you have taught them and helped to practice using before. Then they can frequently do so by asking themselves, "What REBT techniques have I used before to deal with this problem

that I can now use again?" Solution-focused therapy (deShazer, 1985) uses a somewhat similar technique.

5) If new Adversities arise in their lives — or they make them arise — they can use their knowledge of REBT and the profound New Effective Philosophies they have learned by using it to stubbornly refuse to make themselves miserable about almost anything that is likely to plague them during their lives.

6) If using REBT under specially adverse conditions does not seem to be working, they can return to you (or another REBT therapist) for some sessions, to help guide them back to an effective therapeutic groove.

These steps which are discussed in more detail in a journal article (Ellis, 1972), outline the process of using REBT to get and not merely *feel* better. No form of therapy works well for all clients all of the time. But it is hypothesized that REBT, when strongly and persistently used, will help some people reach this "elegant" solution of *getting* better more frequently than will other forms of therapy.

The Reciprocal Influence of Adversities, Beliefs and Consequences (Emotions and Behaviors) on Each Other

As briefly noted before, Adversities (A), people's Beliefs (B) about them, influence and "cause" C, their emotional and behavioral Consequences. A x B=C. But, as also noted, thoughts, feelings, and behaviors are not pure but include and are integrated with each other. Similarly, though REBT especially emphasizes A's and B's influence on C, it also sees A affecting B and C, B affecting A and C, and C affecting A and B.

Rational Emotive Behavior Therapy's
A-B-C Theory of Emotional Disturbance

"People are disturbed not by things, but by the views which they take of them."
— *Epictetus, 1st century A.D.*

It is not the event, but rather it is our *attitudes and beliefs* about it, that causes our emotional reaction.

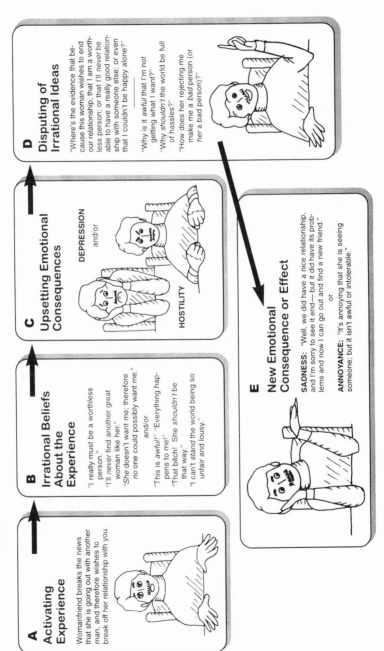

A
Activating Experience

Womanfriend breaks the news that she is going out with another man, and therefore wishes to break off her relationship with you.

B
Irrational Beliefs About the Experience

"I really must be a worthless person."

"I'll *never* find another great woman like her."

"*She* doesn't want me; therefore *no* one could possibly want me."

and/or

"This is *awful!*" "Everything happens to me!"

"That bitch! She *shouldn't* be that way."

"I can't *stand* the world being so unfair and lousy."

C
Upsetting Emotional Consequences

DEPRESSION

and/or

HOSTILITY

D
Disputing of Irrational Ideas

"Where's the evidence that because this woman wishes to end our relationship, that I am a worthless person; or that I'll *never* be able to have a really good relationship with someone else; or even that I couldn't be happy alone?"

"Why is it *awful* that I'm not getting what I want?"
"Why *shouldn't* the world be full of hassles?"

"How does her rejecting me make me a *bad* person (or *her* a bad person)?"

E
New Emotional Consequence or Effect

SADNESS: "Well, we did have a nice relationship, and I'm sorry to see it end—but it did have its problems and now I can go out and find a new friend."

or

ANNOYANCE: "It's annoying that she is seeing someone; but it isn't awful or intolerable."

Jodi resisted looking for a better job largely because of her two Irrational Beliefs: 1) "I must not fail job interviews or else I'm a hopeless loser." 2) "Preparing for and taking job interviews is too hard and requires too much effort. I'll wait till someone offers me a new job." So she decided to change these IBs and go for job interviews. But she also observed that at A (Adversity) she had little education and training for the kind of job she wanted, that good jobs were scarce in her area, and that some employers thought she was too old (age fifty-five) to work very long before she retired. So these hard facts at A influenced her to have negative thoughts at B, and avoidance of interviews at C.

Jodi's job-avoidance (C) also temporarily decreased her anxiety (C) because she couldn't be rejected, but in the long run increased it, because she wasn't able to disconfirm, in practice, the "awfulness" of rejection. In fact, the less she got rejected, the more "awful" she imagined it would be. So her job-seeking avoidance (C) also "confirmed" her Irrational Belief (B), "It's awful to be rejected — as I must not be!"

When Jodi more fully saw the ABCs of her job-avoidance she concluded, "It really is hard for me to get the kind of job I want but if I stop telling myself, 'I must not be rejected,' and accept the fact that often I will be, I really have nothing to lose. I'll stop seeing job-hunting as *too hard,* push myself uncomfortably to do it, get familiar with doing it, and overcome my self-induced great fear of job-seeking." Fully looking at her ABCs helped Jodi actively look for a better job.

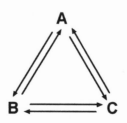

When two or more people relate to each other, their A's not only influence their Bs and Cs, their Bs influence their A's and Cs, and their Cs influence their A's and Bs, but also their A's, Bs, and Cs often affect each other's A's, Bs, and Cs. Bruce and Grace were married and critical of each other. At A (Adversity) Grace took Bruce's criticism, told herself at B (Beliefs about A), "Bruce *must not* criticize me so much! I *can't stand him!*" and made herself enraged at him at C.

Bruce observed Grace's anger (at C) and made it into his Adversity (A). At B, he told himself, "She's always angry and that means I must be doing something wrong. I'm really inadequate!" So at C he felt depressed.

Then Grace observed Bruce's depression (his C) and made it into her Adversity[2] — "I dislike Bruce's being depressed by my anger." She then told herself, "I depressed Bruce with my anger, as I shouldn't have done" (B^2) and she felt, at C^2, guilty.

Bruce then saw Grace's guilt (her C^2)and made it into his A^2, disliking himself for causing Grace guilt. At B^2, he told himself, "I shouldn't make Grace guilty. I'm really a worm for doing so!" At C^2 he felt guilty and more depressed than ever.

Obviously, then, people's ABCs can importantly and reciprocally influence their other A's, Bs, and Cs; and they can affect, and also influence others' A's, Bs, and Cs. They can then *help* disturb, though actually not *directly* disturb, other people, especially ones with whom they are intimate. In relationship therapy, REBT shows couples how they affect each other — but not actually directly disturb each other — as they very often mistakenly conclude (Ellis, 1957; Ellis & Harper, 1961; Ellis, Sichel, diMattia, Yeager, and DiGiuseppe, 1989). It then helps them Dispute their various Irrational Beliefs that largely create their upsetness.

❖ *The Advantages of Active-Directive REBT*

Some disturbed people are thoroughly tired of their dysfunctional feelings and behavior, fully ready to go through the discomforts of changing, and — on their own or with self-help materials — push themselves to change. Fine! — as clients they make good customers. But even though they are bright and constructivist, many change more slowly — or very little. Why? For several reasons:

- They may be biologically prone to be severely disturbed — e.g., have serious personality disorders, and have more trouble doing so than average "nice neurotics."

- They may have low frustration tolerance and won't take the time and the effort usually required of change.

- They may view improvement as "dangerous" because it takes away their excuses for not taking risks that they may fail at.

- They may be more interested in the therapist's approval and continuing therapy with a caring therapist than in getting better and being on their own.

- They may be hostile to others — such as their mates — who push them to change.

- They may not agree with a particular kind of therapy, such as REBT.

- They may have various other reasons for resisting (Ellis, 1985).

When clients resist therapy, it is usually best to refrain from continuing passive methods (forever!), but to actively-directively determine what are their main reasons for resisting, whether they are good reasons (which they may be), and how to help overcome them (if feasible). The theory that if you merely show them their IBs and how to modify them (or otherwise are indirect and less active as a therapist) they will somehow, as constructivists, find their way to good solutions, has very little evidence to back it. Much more evidence shows that active-directive revealing, finding the reasons for, and uprooting clients' resistance often works. If it doesn't, it still may reveal salient reasons for it, and encourage them to use a different form of therapy.

Active-directiveness on your part, moreover, has many other advantages. It shows what will probably be effective for this particular client — who in some ways is different from other clients. It may well work for briefer and effective therapy for some hard-working clients. It helps teach some of the fundamental theories and practices for clients to choose from. Clients are usually in pain when they start therapy and rapport is enhanced by showing them that you can competently guide them into new, less painful ways. Therapy is expensive of the client's time and money and your time and effort, and active-directive (hopefully brief) therapy makes it less expensive. More passive methods of therapy, such as classical analysis and Rogerian person-centered therapy have been shown to "sneak in" directive and subtle reinforcement techniques — because often they alone will work. Many good therapy methods, such as exposure to fearful stimuli and events, have to be directively taught and encouraged. Directiveness emphasizes self-efficacy, which gives clients the confidence they can accomplish many things they are convinced that they cannot do. Directiveness is practically necessary with some clients who have severe personality disorders or other biological or acquired limitations and who require the therapist's activity to push them to overcome these limitations.

REBT, because of these advantages, is usually quite active-directive. But, as a therapist, you had better keep in mind that practically all good things also have disadvantages. Active-directiveness may therefore interfere with your clients' innate proactive tendencies to solve their own problems and to actualize themselves. It may too-strongly present goals and values, and methods to achieve them, that your clients too-suggestibly accept. You may, as a directive therapist, especially in some cases, take over too much responsibility and power, and thereby interfere with a collaborative and cooperative client-therapist relationship.

AE has described several cautions for therapists to take in being overly-directive (Ellis, 1997). These include:

- Be aware of the limitations of the therapy techniques you use.

- Monitor your clients' different reactions to the techniques you recommend and be prepared to stop or modify some of them with individual clients.

- Have many cognitive, emotive, and behavioral methods available, including some more passive methods, which you can at times borrow or steal from other systems of therapy.

- Give unconditional acceptance or Rogers' (1961) unconditional positive regard to all clients and show them how to give it to themselves, so that they neither denigrate themselves nor down themselves when they fail to use your "good" methods.

Caution, caution! The more active-directive you are, the more you may help *and* harm clients. This is particularly true with supersensitive people who are prone to self-denigration. Though you may personally favor active-directive therapy, be careful and always be ready to withdraw. Therapy is often a zigzag instead of a straightly ascending process. Often let it be!

Let us say, in concluding this section, that we have seen some fairly passive, nondirective therapists use REBT and CBT successfully. They go slowly and carefully, because that is their nature. Or, because they passively try to let their clients come to their own conclusions about their IBs, how to Dispute them, and how to feel and act against them. Some REBTers almost exclusively use the Socratic dialogue method of helping clients to question and challenge their IBs. This method, since the therapist uses questions, such as "What did you tell yourself when you were anxious about your procrastination?" and "Is it really true that you must have guaranteed success in presenting your point of view?" is really quite active. But it is hardly as directive as saying, "Didn't you demand that you must present well?" And, "Obviously you don't *have* to present well and would be much less anxious if you only *preferred* to do so."

Again, probably all therapists are *somewhat* active-directive. But as an REBT and CBT practitioner, you have the *choice* of how much to be with individual clients. Try to exert that choice wisely! Discover what works best with this particular client at this time. Experiment!

❖ Summary

- Biological tendencies, environmental conditions, and social conditions all contribute to the reasons that people become upset or disturbed.

- REBT focuses primarily on the cognitive elements of disturbance because changing a core irrational belief can subsequently cause profound improvements emotionally and behaviorally.

- In the "ABC" model of REBT, the "A" is an *activating event* or *adversity* which one experiences in his life such as a situation, person, thought, etc.

- The "C" is the emotional and/or behavioral *consequence* connected to the "A."

- The "B" is the *belief* about the "A," activating event, which actually causes the "C," consequence.

- Beliefs can be rational or irrational. Rational Beliefs (RBs) are flexible, adaptive, consistent with social reality and help us achieve our goals in life. Irrational Beliefs (IBs) are rigid, dogmatic, inconsistent with social reality and generally get in the way of goal attainment.

- REBT focuses on not only helping the client *feel better* in her current situation but also on teaching her to *get better* by using the principles in future situations.

- An active-directive approach to therapy allows for briefer, effective therapy which allows for "teaching" opportunities and can provide added motivation to push the client forward at potentially less expense to the client.

4

The Process of Assessment in REBT

R EBT is somewhat skeptical of rigid diagnostic categories, such as are described in DSM-IV, because they sometimes label people in an overgeneralized way. They may be useful, however, in deciding how severely disturbed your clients are, how long it may take to help them, and what methods may be most useful for individual clients.

Assessment methods that are favored are cognitive-behavioral tests and materials (Kendall & Hollon, 1980), rather than psychodynamic tests, such as the Rorschach test, which are open to many different interpretations. No tests are sacred, because even "objective" tests of clients' acknowledged Irrational Beliefs may be consciously or unconsciously prettified. In our intake packet at the New York Institute, we include some standardized tests as well as forms to collect general biographical data, and prior therapy experience information. We also have clients retake a "satisfaction of life" assessment every four to six weeks to aid in charting progress.

Assessment includes:

1) What are clients' specific cognitive, emotional, and behavioral disturbances and lack of skills (Cs)?

2) What Activating Events or Adversities (A's) commonly accompany their undesirable Consequences (Cs) ?

3) What Rational Beliefs (RBs) and Irrational Beliefs (IBs) tend to evaluate A's and lead to dysfunctional Cs?

4) What cognitive Disputes (D) as well as emotive and behavioral methods are likely to help clients retain their RBs and change their IBs, so that they strongly and persistently arrive at Effective New Philosophies of life (E's)?

5) What thoughts, feelings, and actions will best maintain the clients' progress and preferably help them to actualize and enjoy themselves more?

We usually advocate identifying your client's problematic Consequences (Cs) first as this is the topic that they generally present with and it helps you to assess whether they are feeling/behaving rationally or have irrationally upset themselves over something in their lives. To get the Cs, you can ask, "How do you feel about that?", "How do you physically feel when that happens?", and "What do you do?" Responses to these questions vary greatly and you may have to probe deeper to really understand what's going on in these situations. A client may report that he feels "upset." This is a start, but you want to assess what type of upsetness he is experiencing. Is it anger, depression, jealousy, anxiety, or a combination of things? Is it sadness, frustration, or disappointment? In these cases it may be a rational response. Is your client irrationally overeating when she perceives she is being treated poorly or does she rationally choose not to spend time with the people who don't behave well toward her?

Morgan began his first therapy session by stating that he was upset with his business partner, Bill. When asked about the nature of the upset, he reported feeling anger and disappointment. His disappointment stemmed from not having the kind of working relationship with Bill that he would have liked to have. This was reasonable and based on a desire that wasn't being fulfilled, so we decided to work on the anger because Morgan's anger was unhealthy and was causing him a great deal of stress.

Once you have identified the Cs and have agreed to the most important or pressing Consequence that your client would like to work on, it's time to thoroughly assess the A's (Activating events or Adversities) that precipitate the Consequences. If there are several Cs, you will have to spend some time prioritizing what to work on and in what order. Clients rarely, if ever, experience their upset *all of the time*. Therefore, it is important that you help them to identify the particular situations, people, or thoughts which trigger their unhelpful Consequences. Helpful questions include, "When do you feel/behave that way?", or "Which situations usually result in that Consequence?". You can also have your client relate the most recent experience he had with the Consequences in order to get a sense of the A's.

Morgan became angry with Bill in situations where he believed that Bill was not "pulling his weight" in the office. Recently, Bill had left work early to go to a baseball game instead of staying to finish the day's business. Morgan had not only stayed late to finish the work but had also fumed about it the entire evening and had trouble falling asleep because of his invasive thoughts about Bill's "lazy work ethic." He then behaved abruptly and was unfriendly toward Bill for the next couple of days. Morgan reported that these types of scenarios happened once or twice a week.

The next step is to identify the Bs (Beliefs) which cause the reactions (Cs). Appropriate queries are, "What are you telling yourself when you make yourself (jealous) (depressed) (overeat) etc.?", and "How are you making yourself (angry) (anxious) etc.?", and "What's going through your head while you're feeling/behaving this way?" You will usually elicit both rational and irrational beliefs with these questions. Keep in mind that:

Rational Beliefs (RBs) are those which are healthy, productive, adaptive, and consistent with social reality. They generally consist of preferences, desires, and wants.

Irrational Beliefs (IBs) are rigid, dogmatic, unhealthy, maladaptive, and mostly get in the way of our efforts to achieve our goals. IBs are comprised of demands, musts, and shoulds.

It's your job to work at identifying and positively reinforcing the rational statements (RBs), while taking note of the irrational statements (IBs) which are the beliefs which contribute the most to the unhealthy Cs. The goal is to attempt to uncover hidden demands (shoulds), awfulizing, global self- or other-downing, and low frustration tolerance (I-can't-stand-ititis). You may have to ask several times or many different ways in order to accomplish this task.

Morgan said that when he became angry at Bill his thoughts included, "it's not fair that I have to work so hard and he doesn't," "he's not putting in enough time (as he should)," "he's a real jerk for putting me in this situation," and "I wish I got to take breaks like that." The last statement, again, was healthy and rational. Morgan's desire to take breaks wasn't getting him into any real trouble. It led him to feel disappointed but didn't cause him to feel overly upset or act in any inappropriate ways. The first two beliefs, however, were getting Morgan into a lot of trouble. He was rigidly and irrationally demanding that Bill not be the way he obviously was. He was also globally labeling Bill as a complete "jerk" because of his behavior in this one area. In addition, he was strongly and illogically believing that because he thought Bill should put in more time, he therefore ought to. Finally, he was exhibiting some low frustration tolerance in his belief that he, Morgan, shouldn't have to work so hard.

After identifying the ABCs of a particular Consequence with your client, you can then begin to scrutinize, evaluate, test, and ultimately, hopefully, replace the IBs which have surfaced during this assessment. Chapters 5, 6, and 7 discuss various approaches to use. Of course, since some clients aren't familiar with the ABC model, it may take longer to work through the initial assessments until you begin to feel more comfortable with REBT and your client becomes more knowledgeable about it. One way to facilitate the experience is to discuss the REBT model and theory with your clients at the very beginning of therapy so that they have a basic understanding of it and an opportunity to ask questions if necessary. Often, with experience, clients will begin to present their problems in the ABC format but, as with most things, this comes with practice!

Something else to keep in mind, as in the example of Grace and Bruce in chapter 3, is that Cs can often become A's for your clients. This means that a Consequence can become the trigger for a whole separate ABC assessment and exploring this possibility is equally important in assessing the problem. For example, when Morgan became angry at Bill, he later felt guilty about it and put himself down. Thus, his anger (the C in the first example), became a secondary A in that it led to feeling guilty and self-downing. This was due to self-statements (IBs) like, "I shouldn't have been so mean to Bill," "It's terrible of me to get so angry at a friend," etc. You can assess for secondary problems by asking, "How do you feel about yourself for being (angry) (anxious) (depressed) etc. and/or for behaving like that?". As a rule of thumb, if you find that your client is experiencing secondary or even tertiary upset about the problem, it's best to start with the tertiary (or secondary) upset and work your way back to the primary problem. Incidentally, clients may also initially present what turns out to be a secondary problem as the main problem so it's important to keep asking questions and formulating and testing hypotheses throughout therapy.

Assessment in REBT is an ongoing process. Therapy itself is usually relied upon as the main method of diagnosis. For it is quickly seen, when using REBT, what Adversities (A's) your clients most upset themselves about, what IBs they have about these A's, how accurately they can recognize their IBs, how well and forcefully they Dispute them, what Effective New Philosophies (E's) they devise, etc. You can see the most important aspects of their disturbances and how they use REBT methods to change or not change themselves. You can thus keep teaching and following up on the more effective methods of changing and dropping the less effective methods for each individual client. Moreover, you don't have to stick with favorite REBT techniques but can at times use less favored ones — and even use techniques from other systems that you generally disfavor.

There are no *musts* about using many possible REBT and non-REBT methods — only *preferences* that are guided by their effectiveness with different clients. As Paul (1967, p. 11) has observed, you ask yourself, "*What* treatment, by *whom,* is most effective for *this* individual with *that* specific problem, and under *which* set of circumstances?" As usual, REBT above all is flexible!

Summary

- Assessment is a vital and ongoing element of the therapeutic process.

- The most effective assessments include objective data combined with a client's self-report about biographical background information, previous therapy experience, and a thorough look at the current problem(s).

- It is also important that you assess how much your client knows about the type of therapy you practice because you may need to begin with a description of your theoretical approach.

- Equally important is to evaluate if any secondary, tertiary, etc. problems exist as spin-offs from the primary problem.

5

Cognitive Techniques in REBT

U p to now you've gotten a general overview of the theory and practice of Rational Emotive Behavior Therapy. At this point you may be saying to yourself, "I understand what I'm supposed to be working toward but I still don't know how to get there." Well, relax. You're not the first therapist to think this way. We've often noticed this in our professional training programs. Understanding the basic ideas is fundamental to using this approach successfully but without the actual techniques it will be difficult to get very far.

Because this type of therapy is relatively simple in its theory, therapists sometimes make the mistake of thinking that if they read a book or two about the theory of REBT they *automatically* will be able to practice it successfully with their clients. However, as you probably know from personal experience, *understanding* something and successfully *practicing* it often do not go hand in hand. The next three chapters will be devoted to actual techniques which you can use in therapy to help clients identify, clarify, scrutinize, and replace their unhelpful cognitive, behavioral, and emotive patterns. Keep in mind that just as our thoughts, behaviors, and emotions are interconnected, the following categories are not mutually exclusive. Many of the techniques overlap and could be placed under one of the other headings but we have attempted to place them in the categories which seem to reflect the basic emphasis of the intervention. As a therapist, it's crucial that you practice and experiment with using these interventions so that you are able to integrate them into your own therapeutic style and become comfortable with using them.

There are two things which are important to accomplish before moving into the intervention phase of therapy with your client. First, you have explained the theory and practicalities of the ABC model to your client and you feel confident that she has a basic understanding of it. Second, your client has at least tentatively agreed to work from the premise that she is mainly responsible for her reactions to life's ups and downs. Once you've accomplished those two things, it's time to move on to helping your client implement some changes.

As you read the descriptions of REBT techniques in this and the two following chapters, you may find that you want more information on a particular procedure. We have included some references in the text, and call your attention also to the resource described on page 105, and to the References list, pages 135-162.

❖ *Disputing*

REBT is probably best known for its method of Disputing. This is an active approach for helping clients evaluate the helpfulness and efficacy of elements of their belief systems (Bernard, 1991, 1993; Dryden, 1994; Ellis, 1962, 1973, 1985, 1988; Ellis and Grieger, 1977, 1988, Ellis & Harper, 1975; Walen, DiGiuseppe & Dryden, 1992; Yankura & Dryden, 1990). Once your clients are familiar with the ABCs of REBT, Disputing will allow them to identify, debate, and ultimately replace their rigid, inflexible beliefs which are generally getting them into trouble. You will also be able to show them how to generalize the use of these functional, empirical, and logical challenges to other areas.

You can approach disputing by using a didactic or Socratic style. A didactic approach refers to an informational portion of a session where you, as the therapist, provide an explanation of different terms and may explain the difference between rational and irrational beliefs. As discussed in chapter 4, *Rational Beliefs (RBs)* are flexible, adaptive, help us reach our goals, and are consistent with social reality. *Irrational Beliefs (IBs)* are those which are rigid, dogmatic, cannot be fully supported by social reality, and by and large get in the way of goal achievement. You can also give examples of rational v. irrational beliefs using a didactic approach and posit possible hypotheses about your particular client's beliefs. You may often find that a didactic, "lecturing" style is helpful, especially in the beginning phase of treatment as you start to educate your client about Rational Emotive Behavior Therapy. Later, you will be able to integrate a Socratic, or questioning, approach in order to identify and dispute irrational thinking. A Socratic approach involves a great deal more client involvement. Through a series of leading questions, you are able to pinpoint more specifically how and where your client's thinking, feeling, and behaving is becoming problematic.

The driving force behind disputing is the fact that most of us adopt a belief system about the world which strongly influences our reactions, and that we rarely question these beliefs even though they may be impractical, unrealistic, and illogical. In addition, we often reinforce these beliefs so often that we may be mostly unaware of how powerful they are in our lives. CM had an opportunity to work in a organization several years ago where staff members were encouraged periodically to throw out all of their procedures and then attempt to "argue" them back into policy. If they were able to produce clear, logical, and empirically justifiable reasons to reinstate a particular procedure in the way that they ran the organization, they were allowed to do so. If there was little or no compelling evidence for a procedure then it was tossed out and a new one was formulated to be implemented and tested. This is very similar to what we ask clients to do with certain parts of their belief systems. The first step in effectively disputing is identifying with your client his particular Irrational Belief(s) as discussed in chapter 4. Once you identify that a core irrational or unhelpful belief may have been unearthed, it is your job to aid your client in testing this hypothesis. There are four main ways to do this.

❖ Functional Disputes

The purpose of this intervention is to question the practical applications of some of your client's beliefs and their accompanying emotions and behaviors. Specifically, it entails evaluating it to find out if the particular belief, behavior, or emotion is helping your client get where she wants to go in life. Typical questions are, "Is it helping you?" or "How is continuing to think this way (or behave this way, or feel this way) affecting your life?" The goal of functional disputing is to point out to your client that the belief is getting in the way of her goals. Most often, clients will be able to identify at least one and often several ways that their particular belief (behavior, emotion) is getting them into trouble. A typical functional dispute would be implemented this way:

Ian: "Whenever I see my girlfriend talking to another man I get upset."

Therapist: "Upset in what way?"

Ian: "Well, I start to feel really jealous and I want her to stop talking to him right away."

Therapist: "And you feel jealous because?"

Ian: "She may decide she likes him better than me and leave me."

Therapist: "And what if she did leave you?"

Ian: "I couldn't handle it and my life would be terrible."

Therapist: "And what would it say about you if she left you?"

Ian: "That I'm no good. That there's something wrong with me."

Therapist: "And how does believing that you're no good if she leaves you help you?"

Ian: "I guess it doesn't really help. It makes me feel really upset."

Therapist: "And when you start to feel upset in these situations what do you do?"

Ian: "I usually end up doing something stupid like walking up to Jacqui and making a big deal out of kissing her to show that she's taken or yelling at her and storming out."

Therapist: "And then what?"

Ian: "She gets mad at me and we argue and then I feel guilty and angry at myself."

Therapist: "And your ultimate goal is to stay in the relationship with Jacqui, right?"

Ian: "Yes."

Therapist: "So we've discovered that your belief that you couldn't handle living without her leads you to 1) feel upset in these situations, 2) behave in ways you later regret, and 3) push away the person you're so desperately trying to stay in a relationship with. She becomes upset with you too, right?"

Ian: "Pretty much."

Therapist: "O.K. I'll ask the question again, how is this belief affecting your life?"

Ian: "In a really negative way."

Therapist: "So why would you want to hold onto it?"

Ian: "When you put it that way, I don't."

Through this directed Socratic style of questioning, you are able to help your client to closely scrutinize the beliefs that you suspect, and probably with good evidence, are causing potentially avoidable problems for him.

The reality is that no matter how compelling a functional dispute is, your clients generally won't be able to just toss out a belief overnight. After all, they have most likely been practicing and reinforcing this way of thinking for a very long time. However, what you are trying to do is systematically show them how much they potentially have to gain from working at replacing the Irrational Beliefs with their more flexible, realistic cousins, the Rational Beliefs.

However, there are times when clients will be able to identify *positive consequences* to certain beliefs, behaviors and/or emotions. Jane came to therapy because she was concerned about her extreme anger at her three-year-old child when he had a tantrum. On the one hand, she didn't want to get angry because it scared her child, and because she experienced a "loss of control" over her emotions which was unsettling for her. In addition, she would feel guilty after the fact. These are the reasons she sought counseling. On the other hand, she identified that when she got angry it was a helpful release of tension to her and her child did tend to quiet down faster when she was overtly furious. When presented with a functional dispute, "Is the anger helping you?" her answer was mixed. At that point I asked her, "Is it helping more than it is hurting?" and "Are there other ways to get the positive consequences without getting yourself so upset?" This served two purposes. One was that Jane was able to identify that her anger, in her opinion, was more hurtful than helpful. The second was that we were able to further reinforce her motivation and desire to give up the anger. If there weren't some largely negative consequences to the belief, the client probably wouldn't be seeking help, but sometimes you may have to explore them more fully.

❖ *Empirical Disputes*

The questions in this approach are geared toward evaluating the factual components of your client's belief(s). In other words, testing if the specific belief is consistent with social reality. Often employed questions are "Where is the evidence?", "Where is the proof that this is accurate?", and "Where is it written?". One important thing to remember is that you are not asking why your client would like for it to be the way he is insisting it be or not be. You also are not asking why the majority of people, if polled, might agree with your client. He will probably have many good reasons to want the world to be the way he wants it. However, you are asking for empirical evidence not preferences. Your client will often confuse the question at first and give you preferences.

Here's an example: if you were to ask Ian, the jealous client mentioned in the previous section, for evidence to support his belief that he's no good or worthless without his romantic relationship, he would most likely respond with all of the various reasons losing her would be upsetting and inconvenient for him. He might claim that she would be rejecting him, that she would probably find someone else, or that he would have to look for another relationship. All of these things could be factual and very disappointing for Ian. But the question would still remain as to how losing his relationship with her would make him worthless. Of course, the answer to this question is that there is no evidence that this client's worth as a person would necessarily be compromised, but he has been linking his worth to maintaining this relationship strongly enough and long enough so that he really believes it. Consequently, the prospect of a breakup does seem life threatening to him and causes him to feel and behave in ways that get him in trouble.

Your task with an empirical dispute is to help your client understand that he has been holding onto a belief which is insupportable and when questioned, doesn't make much sense. It is important during this process to support his desires and valid concerns and also to separate the rational concerns from the irrational beliefs and fears.

❖ *Logical Disputes*

Logical disputing is focused on questioning the illogical leap your client is making from desires or preferences to demands in his irrational thinking. Just because he wants something to happen or be a certain way, doesn't mean necessarily that it will. Appropriate questions are, " How does it follow that just because you'd like this thing to be true and it would be very convenient, it *should* be?" and "Where is the logic that Y *must* follow X?" Again, clients may give you many reasons why they would like for it to be true but, ultimately, if the belief is irrational, it will be logically insupportable. Also, you may ask, "How does it follow that failing at an important task makes *you,* a person who may fail at many tasks and succeed at many others, a failure? How does *it,* failing, make *you,* worthless?"

Chuck was depressed over his inability to find the job, romantic relationship, and life of his dreams. At thirty-four, he had been casting around both personally and professionally but never really investing himself fully in anything, "because nothing seems to be *perfect.*" He would either talk himself out of possibilities or half-heartedly engage in jobs, relationships, and projects, only to become disenchanted later *because* he was only halfway involved in them and they didn't fit his ideals of how they *should* be.

The source of his depression was twofold. First, he upset himself about his past by thinking, "I can't stand that I've wasted all this time, it's awful." Then he depressed himself by *awfulizing* about his future. "I'll never get what I want. I'll always be dissatisfied with my life." This, in turn, became something of a self-fulfilling prophecy.

The logical disputes which were useful in this case included, "Where is the logic that a situation must be perfect before you can commit yourself to it?" and "How does it follow that because you haven't enjoyed much success in some areas so far, it will always be that way?" He began to see that much of the problem lay in his attitude and unrealistic demands about his life. He was illogically refusing to invest himself in anything that wasn't "perfect" and making it worse by dooming himself to a miserable future. Once he started to change his beliefs, he was able to make positive changes in his life and to feel more optimistic about the future.

❖ *Philosophical Disputes*

The philosophical approach addresses a life satisfaction issue. Often your client will have been so focused on the identified problem that he has lost perspective on other areas of his life. The problem has subsequently become the defining element of your client's existence. A possible way to address this issue is to ask, "Despite the fact that things will probably not go the way you want some/most of the time in this area, can you still derive some satisfaction from your life?" Often your client's life perspective has become skewed by the problem. It can be helpful to do some reality testing about other aspects of their life that isn't problematic.

Let's look at Jay's situation. He's a thirty-something male who began therapy because he had recently experienced the end of a long-term relationship which he had thought and hoped was "the one." He was not only upset about the breakup but believed that until he had the "right" relationship his overall life satisfaction would be compromised. While supporting him in his desire for and efforts toward a positive, healthy romantic relationship, CM also focused on trying to help him to achieve a sense of life satisfaction without "the relationship." Most of the other areas of Jay's life were quite good. He was healthy, had a strong support system, engaged in activities which he enjoyed, dated frequently, was financially viable, and had a successful career. However, he tenaciously held onto the belief that without a successful, long term romantic relationship, his life was less worthwhile. Suddenly and unexpectedly, he got laid off, due to cut-backs at his workplace. The nature of the therapy sessions changed dramatically. He began to realize how much he had been taking for granted and how well he had been doing aside from the relationship issue. Of course it was unfortunate that something negative had to happen in order for him to gain this perspective but, ultimately, it was quite a good life learning opportunity for him.

Some last comments about Disputing: It's very important to have your clients practice the disputing outside of the stressful situations. When under stress, we revert to our patterned ways of thinking; if they only try disputing when they're in these situations they will have less success. It's not unlike practicing for a sporting event or music recital. A person who has noticed something she wants to change about her performance will usually try to implement the changes by practicing as much as possible — rehearsing outside of games or recitals — in order to be able to perform better in the more important situations. This is true for your client too. Understandably, clients often don't like to focus on problems when they aren't experiencing them. However, they will have a greater chance of success if they do put time aside during non-stressful periods to work on reinforcing and reviewing their Disputing techniques.

❖ *Rational Coping Statements*

Rational coping statement are self-statements which usually are implemented after forceful disputing has been accomplished, but they can also be used while your client is in the process of exploring his beliefs. These factual, encouraging phrases are consistent with social reality and clients are encouraged to repeat them consistently to reinforce the ideas for themselves. They may be encouraging statements such as, "I can accomplish this task," or, "I don't have to get upset in these situations." However, it is preferable to suggest statements which address a deeper philosophical issue as well (Dryden, 1994; Ellis, 1957, 1988; Yankura & Dryden, 1990). For example, "I will work toward accomplishing this task but if I don't succeed it doesn't make me a failure as a person," or, "I don't have to like that he keeps behaving this way but I had better deal with it without demanding that he not be the way he is." All four of the statements above are coping statements but the last two address changing the whole belief system to something more rational instead of simply repeating a positive statement which doesn't address the underlying irrational belief. Through this process your client is beginning to work at rescripting the consistently irrational monologue in his head.

❖ *Modeling*

Modeling can be effective in aiding your client to "get out of her own navel." You can ask her to pick out someone she knows personally or a person or character she may have read or heard about who she admires and would like to emulate. Ask your client to be specific about the person or character's qualities she would like to possess and use the identified person as a reference in sessions.

Jenny mentioned once in session that she wished she could be more like her friend Tom. Jenny began therapy because she had recently ended a two-year romantic relationship and was depressed because she believed she had put off pursuing a lot of interests, pushing herself professionally, and nurturing many of her friendships while she was in the relationship and was now "behind" and afraid that a breakup would happen again if she started another relationship. When CM questioned her about her friend Tom, she said he seemed much more able to maintain a balance in his life even when he was romantically involved. Using Tom as a model, Jenny was able to identify her own unhelpful tendency to become so focused on the relationship that everything else became secondary. Tom, on the other hand, healthily maintained many of the same goals and priorities he had prior to relationships and viewed a romantic relationship as a supplement/ complement to his life instead of an all-defining factor. Therefore it wasn't "devastating" to him if/when a romance ended. Jenny was helped to review many of the differences between Tom's thinking about relationships and her own until she was able to start replacing her irrational thoughts ("I must be loved"; "I'm a failure without a romantic relationship") with more rational thinking.

❖ *Referenting*

Referenting is really just a less formal way of saying "cost benefit analysis". This involves having your clients make lists of the real advantages and disadvantages of changing their irrational thoughts and behaviors. The purpose is to keep your client mindful of the reasons he has chosen to change and to help shore up his motivation to change if it begins to falter in his efforts. It's extremely important that he keep these lists readily available and review them on a regular basis (Danysh, 1974; Ellis & Velten, 1994). It is especially valuable to have clients who are addicted to a harmful habit, such as smoking, write down ten or fifteen disadvantages of their addiction and then intently review them five or ten times a day.

❖ *Cognitive Homework*

Practice, practice, practice! This is the driving philosophy behind giving a cognitive homework assignment. The time between sessions is equally important in facilitating positive changes in your client's life. Ask your client to identify Adversities (A's) during the time outside of sessions, identify his IBs, and actively dispute them to replace them with effective coping statements. After all, he has probably been practicing the irrational processes for many years. You will find the REBT homework sheets useful for this assignment (see page 70, REBT Homework Sheet).

REBT Self-help Form

A (ACTIVATING EVENTS OR ADVERSITIES)

- Briefly summarize the situation you are disturbed about (what would a camera see?)
- An A can be internal or external, real or imagined.
- An A can be an event in the past, present, or future.

C (CONSEQUENCES)

Major unhealthy negative emotions:

Major self-defeating behaviors:

Unhealthy negative emotions include:

- Anxiety
- Depression
- Shame/Embarassment
- Rage
- Hurt
- Low Frustration Tolerance
- Jealousy
- Guilt

IB.s (IRRATIONAL BELIEFS)

To identify IB.s, look for:

- DOGMATIC DEMANDS (musts, absolutes, shoulds)
- AWFULIZING (It's awful, terrible, horrible)
- LOW FRUSTRATION TOLERANCE (I can't stand it)
- SELF/OTHER RATING (I'm / he / she is bad, worthless)

D (DISPUTING IB.S)

To dispute ask yourself:

- Where is holding this belief getting me? Is it helpful or self-defeating?
- Where is the evidence to support the existence of my irrational belief? Is it consistent with social reality?
- Is my belief logical? Does it follow from my preferences?
- Is it really awful (as bad as it could be?)
- Can I really not stand it?

E (EFFECTIVE NEW PHILOSOPHIES)

To think more rationally, strive for:

- NON-DOGMATIC PREFERENCES (wishes, wants, desires)
- EVALUATING BADNESS (it's bad, unfortunate)
- HIGH FRUSTRATION TOLERANCE (I don't like it, but I can stand it)
- NOT GLOBALLY RATING SELF OR OTHERS (I—and others—are fallible human beings)

E (EFFECTIVE EMOTIONS & BEHAVIORS)

New healthy negative emotions:

New constructive behaviors:

Healthy negative emotions include:

- Disappointment
- Concern
- Annoyance
- Sadness
- Regret
- Frustration

Bibliotherapy/Psychoeducational Assignments

You can supplement your therapy contacts with bibliotherapy/ psychoeducational assignments to further reinforce the work you are doing in sessions. Assigning helpful audio cassettes, videos, pamphlets, books, lectures, workshops, and topic specific groups can all contribute to your client's understanding of her problems and progress in changing inappropriate and unhelpful reactions. Review any material you assign to your client to assess its helpfulness and to allow you to be prepared to answer questions or concerns about the assignment.

Proselytizing

Encouraging your client to try to help friends and relatives deal with their irrational beliefs can often help them to more effectively address their own problems (Ellis & Abrahms, 1978). As we all have probably experienced as therapists, it is often easier to dissect someone else's problem. It can be a less threatening way of identifying IBs and then the outcome can be used to generalize to your client's problems. An important cautionary note with this intervention is to alert your client to the fact that he may not always receive positive reactions to his proselytizing. Advocating a moderate approach is certainly key, as is encouraging your client to pay attention to social cues that indicate that he's not being well received. Even if he isn't well received by many others, you can at least address his insights into others' problems in the session.

Recently, CM ran a six week assertiveness training group. In the sixth session, one of the participants stated that she had originally been taken aback by some of the overgeneralizing statements another participant had made during the group about men and lawyers. She then added, "But I've been thinking about it and I've realized that I'm glad she's been saying those things. I think I have a tendency to say those same types of things to myself but it's much easier to hear how ridiculous it sounds when someone else says it! Overgeneralizing doesn't help me deal well with other people and I'm committed to changing that!"

❖ Recording Therapy Sessions

At the Institute we often keep tape recorders in our offices for just this reason. As you have probably experienced, it's extremely difficult to recall everything that happens in sessions with clients (a good reason to take notes). For a client who is slogging through a lot of different issues, taping the session for her to listen to again can be very effective (Ellis & Abrahms, 1978; Ellis & Velten, 1992). Your client will often pick up additional helpful aspects the more she listens to the tape, and it can reinforce the content of the session. It can also be an opportunity for her to really listen to herself and pinpoint the thinking that gets her into trouble. After listening to their therapy sessions, clients will sometimes report that they felt they were listening to someone else, which helped them be a little more objective about the content of what was being said.

❖ Reframing

This is a technique used in a variety of therapeutic approaches to aid clients in gaining perspective on their problems. You can encourage your client to look for problems that may include some positive aspects also. At the very least, they may be able to see negative A's as opportunities to practice the tools they have learned in therapy. Instead of viewing the A's in threatening, absolutistic, negative ways, they may be able to accept them as a challenge to be appropriately overcome (Ellis, 1965, 1985, 1988).

❖ *Stop and Monitor*

This is an assignment for between sessions. CM first learned of this technique from Professor Donald Krill in the Graduate School of Social Work at the University of Denver, and has found it to be extremely helpful with clients. This is particularly useful with clients who have a difficult time identifying their thoughts. Because we talk to ourselves so often internally, we can become oblivious to the messages that we repeat and beat ourselves with in our heads. In fact, depending on your client's previous experiences, this may be one of the first times he has considered the possibility that he may be his own worst enemy.

Ask your client to set up unobtrusive cues for himself in everyday places. For example, CM affixed a piece of yellow tape to the dashboard of her car when given this assignment. Other possibilities are a computer monitor, desk calendar, medicine cabinet, etc. Every time the client notices this cue, he is immediately to take note of the thoughts that have been going through his head. Sometimes these will be just neutral, everyday thoughts like, "I have to go grocery shopping" or "The subway (highway) was crowded this morning." However, the thoughts that you are most interested in are the negative, evaluative, irrational thoughts which may be identified during the course of this exercise. They may have become so commonplace in your client's mind that he is hardly aware of them. These should be noted and discussed in session. Clients are often surprised at the content and negativity in some of their thinking and this can be a great way to start and/or reinforce the process of change.

❖ *Summary*

The three main purposes of cognitive techniques are to identify, challenge, and actively replace irrational thinking. The initial and primary focus of REBT is on the cognitive processes because philosophic changes in the way a client thinks can have lasting positive effects on emotions and behaviors as well.

6

Emotive/Experiential Techniques in REBT

Emotive/Experiential techniques are used to supplement and reinforce the cognitive interventions used in REBT. Emotive techniques shift the focus of attention from identifying Irrational Beliefs (IBs) toward further facilitating and enhancing positive shifts in thinking which have been gained through cognitive techniques.

❖ Rational Emotive Imagery

Rational Emotive Imagery (REI) is one of the core emotive/experiential techniques used in the REBT approach. The first purpose of REI is to help your client to identify the more appropriate and rational emotion(s) she would like to feel in problematic situations. The second is to allow your client to explore experientially the self-statements and coping mechanisms which are most compelling and natural for her, and then to practice them with REI until they occur more easily and readily in stressful situations.

Here's how: Ask your client to close her eyes and place herself in a recent difficult situation in which she experienced the extreme, dysfunctional emotion upon which you have mutually agreed to focus. Have her cue you when she has reconstructed in imagination both the situation and the emotional upset. Ask her to label her upsetting feelings (i.e. anxiety, anger, etc.). Then ask her to focus on changing the upset to a more reasonable, healthy negative emotion. Have her cue you when she has accomplished this. Then invite her to gradually return to the present and to open her eyes. The first question to ask her is, "How did you end up feeling?" Take note of her answer. Then ask her what she did to be able to change her upset. It is important that you take note of her specific wording. You can also explore how her thoughts helped her to feel more healthily instead of unhealthily upset.

Here is a recent example of using REI with Liz who becomes enraged at her boss when he makes "stupid" statements:

Therapist: "If you would, sit back and close your eyes. O.K., now I want you to put yourself in a recent situation, maybe the one we talked about today, where Tom said something you thought was really stupid. Let me know when you feel the anger. Really feel it! Feel it!"

10-second pause.

Liz: "I'm feeling angry, very angry."

Therapist: "Now I'd like for you to focus on your anger and change it to a less upsetting, more adaptable feeling. Feel sorry and annoyed but *not* angry. Let me know when you get there."

Liz: Laughs. "That's going to be a stretch."

Therapist: "I know. Focus on the anger and the situation and really work at changing your anger to feeling sorry and annoyed but *not* angry. Take your time."

20-minute pause.

Liz: "O.K."

Therapist: "Now bring your thoughts back to this room and open your eyes. How did you end up feeling?"

Liz: "Annoyed. A little frustrated."

Therapist: "Can you describe that a little more?"

Liz: "Uncomfortable, but better than being really angry."

Therapist: "And what did you do to feel annoyed instead of angry?"

Liz: "I thought that this doesn't have to bother me so much. I told myself that getting angry wasn't going to change him and that it was just giving control over my emotions to him. I also thought that I don't have to like this, or him, but I can deal with it."

Therapist: "That's great! Why do you think saying those things helped you feel less upset?"

Liz: "Probably because I wasn't taking him so seriously. I wasn't screaming inside my head that he's unbelievable and I can't take it like I usually do."

It's important for you to prescribe healthy instead of unhealthy emotions for your client during REI but, allow her to define them for herself as much as possible. You want her to distinguish clearly between healthy and unhealthy negative feelings and to change the latter to the former. If your client has already stated a healthy emotion she would like to feel instead before you begin the REI, then it is O.K. to supply it as the goal emotion. Otherwise it's best to prescribe a healthy emotion that will feel genuine so that thereafter she will automatically feel that one instead of the unhealthy one she is used to feeling.

REI is often assigned to clients for practice every day for about thirty days. The purpose is to have them become more adept at changing the unhealthy negative emotions so that they are able to draw on the thoughts more easily when they are in a stressful real-life situation. REI is very effectively assigned for homework in conjunction with *reinforcements and penalties* (see chapter 7).

Forceful Coping Statements

This is an opportunity to increase the effectiveness of rational coping statements as discussed in the previous chapter by adding an emotive element to it. In addition to formulating the rational statements, have your client practice them powerfully and forcefully during and between sessions (Bernard and Wolfe, 1993; Ellis, 1996; Ellis, 1985, 1988; Ellis & Abrahms, 1978, Ellis and Velten, 1992). Your client has most likely been practicing the unhealthy, irrational statements consistently and strongly for quite a while, so your task is to get her to do the same with the rational, healthy statements. For example, "When I fail it NEVER NEVER makes me 'a complete failure' as a person." Have your client yell out her rational self-statements or have her stand up and say the statements strongly over and over again.

Forceful Taped Disputing

In addition to the helpfulness of taping sessions, as we discussed in chapter 5, and practicing emotively forceful coping statements discussed above, taping forceful disputing can combine the effect of all of these and further strengthen the helpful, rational "voice." The way that CM often explains this to clients is to point out that they have been strongly and sometimes passionately practicing their irrational ways of thinking for quite some time. Therefore, calmly and unemotionally practicing their disputes may not counteract the other, more compelling and forceful, unhelpful beliefs.

❖ *Role Playing*

The first step in role playing is for you and your client to identify a previously upsetting or potentially upsetting interaction with another person that your client would like to handle more effectively. In basic role playing the client plays himself and your role is to portray the other person, as he or she has been described by your client. You then begin to converse in your "roles." Generally, your client has a specific scenario which he would like to work on or which seems to facilitate more problems for him. This is the scenario to role play with him. Role plays can last from one to five minutes, depending on the situation. After you have completed it, ask your client how he thinks it went, what he was thinking during it, what he was feeling, and if there is anything he would have liked to have done differently. You may identify irrational beliefs which you'll want to take some time to explore, dispute, and replace (see *Disputing*, chapter 5). This is also an opportunity for you to give him feedback about how he came across during the interaction. You can role play the same situation many times, making changes or exploring different possibilities as you go along.

Essentially, you are placing your client in a superficially similar situation and assisting him to experience or handle it in a more adaptive, functional way. This provides a less threatening atmosphere for your client to explore possible cognitive, emotive, or behavioral blocks and experiment with various solutions to future interactions. The therapy session becomes a testing ground for the interpersonal experiences your client has outside of sessions. Previous situations can be role played to prepare for similar future situations. The advantage, of course, is that the client has as many opportunities as he wants to practice and you are available to provide feedback on his approach. At times, some social skills training may be appropriate. For example, something as simple as using "I" statements may make a difference in how your client presents himself. Role playing is especially useful in conjunction with assertiveness training and anger management issues. It also can be implemented in couples counseling. In those cases, you are less active in the role play because each partner plays himself or herself but the feedback process afterward is the same. More information on role playing can be gained by reading *The Essential J.L. Moreno*, Moreno, J.L. (1990) New York: Springer.

❖ *Reverse Role Playing*

Reverse role playing is different from role playing in several ways. First, you take on the role of your client. Second, your client becomes either the therapist (you) or the other person with whom she would like to communicate more effectively. More often she is asked to take on the role of the therapist. Third, although the exercise can sometimes be used for you to model the client's role for him in the identified scenario, more often reverse role playing is used to help the client specifically dispute her own irrational beliefs. As you and your client switch roles, she is now in a position to actively dispute her own irrational beliefs, which you adopt and hold onto as strongly as she has in earlier sessions. This can be very useful with clients who seem to be struggling with disputing their IBs or those who seem to do it lightly and without much conviction.

❖ *Humor*

We humans tend to take ourselves and our fallibility too seriously at times. Certainly there are times when we had better take things seriously, but you can encourage your client to lighten up on herself and see that some of her beliefs are actually funny when taken to extremes. Of course, you want to focus on making light of some of her beliefs and behaviors, not her as a person. Through exaggeration and comparisons you can bring appropriate silliness and fun into your sessions while addressing serious problems.

Jessie, a group member and accomplished lawyer, recently stated that she feels guilty after eating because she believes she is unacceptably overweight and therefore *shouldn't* eat. Upon further questioning, Jessie was able to identify an even more extreme belief that "only thin people deserve to eat." She and the group members laughed at the self-defeating and irrational nature of this belief. "Alert the press," someone said, "there are a lot of non-thin people out there who should know about this!" No wonder any consumption of any kind of food caused upset for her! She had placed herself in a lose/lose situation with her nutty thinking. Of course, humor may not always be appropriate with certain clients and you have to use your best judgement when using it (much like any style or intervention). As a rule of thumb, if humor naturally finds its way into a session, it's usually appropriate.

Another form of humor and attempt to take life a little less seriously comes in the form of rational humorous songs which we use at the Institute in New York and in our training programs around the world. Clients can also be assigned to sing these to themselves. Here are some examples which you can use in sessions with your clients:

PERFECT RATIONALITY

(Tune: "Funiculi, Funicula" by Luigi Denza)

Some think the world must have a right direction,
And so do I — and so do I!
Some think that, with the slightest imperfection
They can't get by — and so do I!
For I, I have to prove I'm superhuman,
And better far than people are!
To show I have miraculous acumen —
And always rate among the Great!
Perfect, perfect rationality
Is, of course, the only thing for me!
How can I ever think of being
If I must live fallibly?
Rationality must be a perfect thing for me!

LOVE ME, LOVE ME, ONLY ME!

(Tune: "Yankee Doodle Dandy")

Love me, love me, only me
Or I'll die without you!
Make your love a guarantee
So I can never doubt you!
Love me, love me totally — really, really try dear;
But if you demand love, too
I'll hate you till I die, dear!
Love me, love me all the time
Thoroughly and wholly!
Life turns into slushy slime
'Less you love me solely!
Love me with great tenderness
With no ifs or buts, dear.
If you love me somewhat less,
I'll hate your goddamned guts, dear!

YOU FOR ME AND ME FOR ME
(Tune: "Tea for Two" by Vincent Youmans)
Picture you upon my knee
Just you for me, and me for me!
And then you'll see
How happy I will be, dear!
Though you beseech me
You never will reach me —
For I am autistic
As any real mystic!
And only relate to
Myself with a great to-do, dear!
If you dare to try to care
You'll see my caring soon will wear,
For I can't pair and make our sharing fair!
If you want a family,
We'll both agree you'll baby me —
Then you'll see how happy I will be!

I WISH I WERE NOT CRAZY!
(Tune: "Dixie" by Dan Emmett)
Oh, I wish I were really put together —
Smooth and fine as patent leather!
Oh, how great to be rated innately sedate!
But I'm afraid that I was fated
To be rather aberrated —
Oh, how sad to be mad as my Mom and my Dad!
Oh, I wish I were not crazy! Hooray! Hooray!
I wish my mind were less inclined
To be the kind that's hazy!
I could, of course, agree to be less crazy —
But I, alas, am just too goddamned lazy!

How to Become a Better Procrastinator

1) Devoutly believe that if you avoid unpleasant situations and problems they will probably disappear.

2) Assume you can't change things — one's life is controlled by outside situations and people.

3) Never take a risk or chance in life.

4) Demand the approval of just about everyone in your life — and even a few who are not.

5) Assume failure or rejection is the worst thing that can happen and that you can't stand it.

6) Demand to be 100 percent competent in everything you do — demand perfection. Put yourself down if you don't achieve it.

7) Assume you can't stand discomfort because life should be easy and fair, at least for you. Upset yourself every time life is uneasy or unfair.

8) Say over and over "everything will be all right" without doing anything about it.

9) Don't put any significant amount of effort into working on your problems.

10) Find a terrific reason for justifying why you are the way you are and refuse to give it up.

11) Say "if only" over and over but, again, do nothing about it.

12) Operate on the assumption that because you procrastinated, failed, and screwed up in the past, you must continue to do so in the future.

13) Believe in the Myths of Change such as:
    a) I'm too old
    b) It's too hard
    c) This is the way I am
    d) Things will probably improve by themselves
    e) I'm too weak (stupid, unmotivated, etc.) to change by myself

14) Rationalize
    a) I will start tomorrow (mañana attitude)
    b) The cavalry will be here on time
    c) Pleasure lost is never regained

15) Just think about the problem and wait for the moment of inspiration to occur before doing anything.

Unconditional Acceptance by Therapist

Part of your job as a therapist is to model positive, helpful attitudes and beliefs for your client whenever possible. One way to accomplish this is to practice giving your client unconditional acceptance — or, as Carl Rogers called it, *unconditional positive regard* — no matter how badly or self-defeatingly they behave (Rogers, 1961). Depending on the client, this can certainly be challenging at times but if you want her to succeed at increasing her USA or unconditional self-acceptance, modeling unconditional acceptance will be very helpful in the process. Of course, this is not to say that if your client becomes abusive or behaves badly that you have to embrace and like the behavior. We don't want your clients to be able to use you as a punching bag! However, you can assertively set limits with her and reject her behavior without condemning her as a person.

Teaching Unconditional Self-Acceptance (USA) and Unconditional Other Acceptance (UOA)

In addition to modeling unconditional acceptance for your client, it is vital that you also actively teach the theory and practice of USA and UOA. A crucial element to teaching this concept is reinforcing the philosophy that humans cannot be rated entirely by any one or group of behaviors or characteristics which comprise their existence. Certain characteristics and behaviors can certainly be rated but when you *behave badly* how can it possibly make you, *as a whole person,* bad or worthless? *Being entirely bad would mean that every single aspect of who you are, and have been, has been all, 100 percent bad since the beginning of your existence.*

Unfortunately, most of us are accustomed to labeling our entire selves and others negatively when we do things we regret or notice aspects of others which we don't like. Interestingly, it's much less frequent that humans label themselves globally worthwhile when they recognize some *positive* aspect of themselves! We don't advocate either of those options. You'd better identify, and help your clients to identify for themselves, behaviors which they don't like, and make strides to change them while accepting themselves as fallible humans in the process. But if they condemn themselves as a person based on these flaws instead of focusing on the particular behavior or trait, they'll greatly inhibit their ability to change those things. The same goes for their perceptions of others. They can certainly rationally decide not to associate with some people, but if they rate them globally based on specific traits they'll be perpetuating the same irrationality that they use against themselves!

You will probably have to address the "myth of guilt" with your clients also. Many people believe that it's important to feel guilty or "bad" about our behaviors because this will lead to positive change. The problem is that while regret is helpful, guilt will often result in engaging in the same kinds of self-defeating and self-sabotaging behaviors. Regret is looking back on a situation and assessing that you would have liked to have behaved differently. *Regret is rating the act as bad.* Guilt is combining regret with a lot of self-downing. In other words, it's not only regretting something but *labeling your entire self as worthless or "bad"* for having behaved the way you did. If I see myself as entirely "bad" or "worthless," there's a good chance I will continue to behave as I think a "bad" or "worthless" person would, thus continuing negative patterns and building up more evidence against myself. *Condemn the act but not the person!*

❖ *Encouragement*

As highly interactive therapists, we often tend to think that providing encouragement for our clients is a natural part of the therapeutic relationship. After all, encouragement is generally supposed to come naturally to those of us who choose a "helping" profession. However, we may sometimes forget that encouragement is important not only in promoting change but in acknowledging it also. CM recently met with a client who has worked diligently for many months at realizing his goals. We reviewed the areas which he still recognizes as sometimes problematic for him, emphasizing the positive aspects of implementing new strategies in his thinking and underlining his potential for change. Near the end of the session he said, "I know that it's important to work on these things but I also feel that I have worked hard in other areas," and proceeded to outline the accomplishments he had made so far.

CM: "He was right of course, and I readily agreed with him. What I realized though, and what I proceeded to discuss with him, was that I had been so focused on trying to help him move forward that I had neglected to reinforce and congratulate him on the strides he had made. While we both acknowledged that *rationally* he didn't *need* my validation of his successes, it did make a positive contribution to his progress and motivation in therapy."

❖ *Encounter Exercises*

Encounter exercises are experiential processes which are often used to elicit and address cognitive, emotive, and behavioral issues during a session. These types of exercises are usually used in group and workshop settings because they require more than just one person.

For example, in the Improving Interpersonal Skills workshop at the Institute, we often have group members move around the room interacting with each other based on an emotion or trait that others' have taped to their backs. Members are not aware of what is written on the card affixed to their back. One card may read "angry," others may say "shy" or "funny" or "depressed." After several minutes of interacting with each other, group members return to their seats and are asked to try to identify what the cards on their backs say. Once they have correctly identified their "traits" or "emotions," they are asked to process the experience of being treated as they were during the exercise. The purpose of this encounter exercise is to explore social cues and interpersonal communications.

There are a wide variety of experiential exercises we use in our ongoing groups, special all-day marathon groups, and nine-hour intensives, including exercises geared toward showing warmth, overcoming fear, being helpful, sharing secrets, and practicing assertiveness, intimacy and empathy. These give participants an opportunity to explore areas which may be problematic and to begin to learn new skills with which to navigate their lives. A few samples of the exercises appear on the next page.

Suggested Exercises for Group Settings

LEARNING FROM MISTAKES: Think of a situation which you did not handle well. Close your eyes and bring up the feelings and thoughts you had at the time. Open your eyes and jot them down. Share them with the group and let them help to identify any thought distortions. What would you like to have happened? Develop a list of rational beliefs and coping statements which might have been helpful.

DEAR DR. RATIONAL: Each person writes a brief letter about one of their problems, as though they were writing to Dear Abby; letters are traded around the room and each person answers someone else's letter — in writing — by using the rational thinking they have been developing.

COMPREHENSIVE SELF-INVENTORY: Have each person use paper and pencil to assess their strengths and weaknesses; have them star the weaknesses which they think might be remediable.

EVIDENCE AGAINST IBs: On one side of an index card write Irrational Beliefs. One the other side, write five negative things that have happened to you because you think this way. Make yourself read the card several times a week to remind yourself how that belief is not working for you.

ANONYMOUS DISPUTING: People pass Irrational Beliefs on a piece of paper to the leader. The leader reads them out and the group as a whole provides counters for them. The rule is that if you agree with the Irrational Belief, you have to keep your mouth shut and listen.

INTRODUCTION EXERCISE: Have individuals finish each sentence, "One thing I'm hoping to gain personally from this meeting........" "One thing I'm hoping to gain professionally from this meeting........"

ROUND OF APPLAUSE: Have participants applaud something or someone they are grateful for. Leader continues to lead standing ovations, whistles, cheering for positive things/people.

HOTSEAT: One at a time, members take the "seat" and as many other participants as want to give feedback. Person remains silent. (Variation: Each participant gives positive feedback and constructive criticism to each hotseat person.).

POSITIVE TALK: Each member is asked to talk positively about himself for a full 2 minutes. (If he qualifies or modifies what he says, he gets a penalty of an additional 30 seconds.)

7

Behavioral Techniques in REBT

imilar to emotive techniques, behavioral interventions and assignments are used to support the cognitive gains made through disputing and replacing the Irrational Beliefs our clients have about their lives and the world. Many of the behavioral techniques are the hands-on practice and reality testing which are needed to reinforce and "prove" the insights that clients have begun to experience in their thinking patterns.

❖ Reinforcements

Behavioral reinforcements are behaviors or pleasure tasks which you work out with your client in conjunction with a "work" task between sessions. They are a fundamental part of collaborating on giving homework assignments to your client after each session. The reinforcement can be anything that your client finds enjoyable which is not harmful to her or to anyone else. Assignments which have reinforcements attached to them stand a greater chance of being completed. The reinforcements add a positive component to the assignments, helping to decrease your client's potential negative thinking about having to carry out the assignment.

Mary is a twenty-four-year-old teacher who is seeing you for help with her overreaction to student misbehavior in class. You want her to practice Rational Emotive Imagery once a day, and to fill out an REBT Self-Help form whenever she experiences a very upsetting situation. (Whatever the assignment, it is important that you specify the desired frequency also. It is easier to implement the reinforcement if you have agreed to a set frequency for the "work" assignment.)

Once you have agreed on the "work" assignment, you will want to explore some of the things your client generally enjoys doing on a regular basis. You learn that Mary likes to read, play computer games, and take long, luxurious baths. Choose one of the options and then explain to Mary that her therapy homework assignment is to earn the right to engage in the chosen reinforcement, by first completing the assigned "work" task. For instance, if she agrees to a daily practice of REI then you can say, "Mary, you are only allowed to take a long bath on the days you practice the REI." It is a bit trickier for assignments like filling out an REBT Self-Help form when upsetting situations happen but you can still say, "Mary, on days when you do have something very upsetting happen, you are allowed to play a half-hour of computer games only after you have filled out a self-help form about the incident."

Reinforcements can also be assigned with *penalties* (see next section) to further enhance the positive consequences of completing the "work" task for your client.

Reinforcements should be generally comparable in time and resources to the "work" assignment you have given your client. If she puts aside twenty minutes each day to mindfully practice her disputing and is then rewarded by reading five pages of a book, it probably won't seem like much of a reinforcement for the time spent disputing. By the same token, being allowed to pamper herself for three hours at the spa for every twenty minutes of daily disputing would not be reasonable either based on the time and resources required to fulfill it each time. Moderation is the key. Rewarding her with an entire chapter of a book or twenty minutes on the phone with friends would be more appropriate and reasonable.

❖ *Penalties*

Behavioral penalties are assigned in much the same way as reinforcements. The difference is that they are assessed as a result of your client *not* completing her homework assignment. A penalty usually consists of a task that your client has identified as unpleasant. She may dislike cleaning the bathroom or sorting the recyclables. Each time that she does not complete the assigned homework, she has to perform the unpleasant penalty task that you have given her. When Ted was attempting to give up smoking he was given the penalty of writing out a $20 check to tobacco lobbyists each time he did not complete his homework assignment. Barbara was told to call up a boring and obnoxious acquaintance and stay on the phone for twenty minutes each time she failed to comply with the mutually agreed upon homework assignment.

When used in conjunction with a *reinforcement* a penalty can be even more onerous; the client must engage in the penalty and forego the reinforcement.

Penalties and reinforcements can usually only be used with highly motivated clients. If your client seems to be struggling with just getting to therapy sessions, let alone completing assignments outside of therapy, then this intervention may be not be appropriate for her. In fact, it may just contribute to an overall sense of failure if used with certain clients.

❖ Shame Attacking Exercises

This intervention is another of the "trademarks" of REBT and is best described by AE in *Better, Deeper, and More Enduring Brief Therapy* (Ellis, 1996 pp 91-94):

I realized, soon after I started doing REBT in 1955, that what we call "shame" is the essence of a great deal of our emotional disturbance. Because when we do something that we consider "shameful," we normally criticize our acts and tell ourselves, "That is bad. I'd better stop doing this and prevent myself from doing it again." We then feel sorry, regretful, or uncomfortable about doing this "shameful" thing, and we help ourselves refrain from repeating it. So defining one or more of our acts or behaviors as "shameful" is often useful; and our human tendency to experience this kind of act-directed shame has helped to socialize us, to prevent us from doing "wrong" or "antisocial" actions, and to probably help to preserve our communities and the human race. Unless we naturally and easily sometimes felt shame, embarrassment, humiliation, and similar emotions, about some of our actions, we would not tend to follow many useful and self-preservative rules and would get into fairly steady trouble.

However, partly because of the human tendency to overgeneralize, just about all of us — including you and your clients — tend not only to rate our deeds, acts, and performances (Good!) but also to rate and measure our selves, our being, our personhood (Incorrect and inefficient!). That is what we do with shame: label our foolish and antisocial acts as "rotten" but also, when we really feel ashamed, measure our entire selves as "rotten" or "shameful." Seeing this, I created my now famous shame-attacking exercise in 1968; and perhaps millions of people, especially psychotherapy clients, have done this exercise and trained themselves to feel ashamed or sorry about what they did, and about the public disapproval that often went with it, but *not* to put themselves down and not to feel humiliated about their personhood.

I explained this shame-attacking exercise to Chana as follows:

"In REBT we try to help people to stop putting themselves, their whole person, down no matter how badly they behave and no matter how much other people look down on them for so behaving. In your case, one of the reasons for your panic about tests is that you know full well that other people — your parents, your teachers, your schoolmates — will discover how badly you do on such tests, and perhaps how panicked you are about taking them, and will view you as an incompetent or a lesser person for your poor performances. So you are not only afraid or ashamed of *your* knowing about your test-taking problem but about *other people* knowing as well. And that is all right as long as you merely try to do well and win people's approval without convincing yourself that you absolutely, under all conditions, *have to* perform adequately and that if you don't, especially if other people see that you don't, your failure and their perceiving this failure make you an RP — a rotten person. Right?"

"Yes," Chana answered, "I just about always rate myself as well as my failings, and particularly feel ashamed, or as you say down myself, when others rate me badly, too."

"Right. Well, this shame-attacking exercise that I am going to encourage you to do will help you forego your *self*-rating and only rate or measure your *performance*. By regular social standards, the latter may indeed be 'poor' or 'inept.' But you are never *a poor or inept person*."

"Even if I do some very bad acts, such as cruelly kill some people?"

"No, *not* even then. Your acts, under those conditions, would be evil and shameful. But you would still be a *person* who behaved badly, and never, really, a bad person."

"But suppose that I usually or practically always do evil acts? Wouldn't I then be a pretty bad person?"

"Yes, you could define yourself as such and call yourself, your entire being, bad. But actually and technically, a 'bad person' would *always* do bad acts, would be undeserving of any satisfaction in his or her life, and would be damnable to the universe. These, again, are either overgeneralizations or unprovable and unfalsifiable propositions. So we'd better not uphold them."

"But how do I stop viewing myself as a totally bad individual?"

"By using several REBT methods. But let's, right now, try a shame-attacking exercise."

"Okay."

"Think of something that you really consider shameful. Something that you normally wouldn't do in front of other people and that, if somehow you did do it, you would feel quite ashamed of doing. Now don't think of or imagine anything that would harm you: Such as walking naked on the street and getting arrested. Or telling one of your professors that she is a real shit. And don't do anything that would harm someone else — such as slapping someone in the face or telling lies about them. Think of something 'shameful,' like telling someone that you just got out of the mental hospital. Or doing a jig on the sidewalk. Or trying to borrow a hundred dollars from a total stranger. Something that almost anyone, including you, would consider shameful but that would not get you or anyone else into any kind of trouble."

"You mean like the famous REBT shame-attacking exercise that I've heard about: yelling out the stops on the subway or on a bus and then staying on the train or bus."

"Yes, that's one of our mainstays, which many of my clients have tried and benefited by. Do you want to try that one?"

"No, I don't think so. But how about my asking a stranger for even a dollar bill. I would be quite ashamed to do that."

"Fine. Let's get you to try that one. Go out on the street, right in front of the Institute if you want, or any place else, and try to borrow a dollar from a stranger. But that's only the first part, the easy part."

"What's the second and harder part?"

"While asking a stranger for a dollar bill, work on yourself to *not* feel ashamed. Work on your possible feelings of embarrassment and humiliation — which you choose to feel but don't have to feel — and make yourself feel unashamed and unembarrassed."

"Is it all right for me to feel uncomfortable?"

"Yes, that will be fine. Feel uncomfortable, sorry, regretful, a bit foolish, or even ashamed of your intruding on the stranger. But not guilty, self-downing, or really ashamed of *yourself*."

"Can I really do that?"

"Of course you can! Try it and see!"

Chana at first hesitated and only did this shame-attacking exercise a week later, just before she came to her therapy session. She kept telling herself that she would be too uncomfortable doing it; and she might never have done it at all had she not had a regularly scheduled therapy session when I would ask her about doing it. But she finally bucked up her courage and did it.

"How did you feel while doing the exercise?" I asked Chana.

"Oh, very uncomfortable at first. I could hardly get the words out of my mouth. I was practically tongue-tied. And the first time I did it my mouth was so dry that the person I picked, a very respectably dressed man walking outside the Waldorf Astoria Hotel, couldn't hear what I had to say. So I very uncomfortably had to repeat it."

"And then?"

"Then I did what I thought I heard you telling me to do: I said to myself, 'He probably thinks I'm a perfect nut. Or maybe one of the dirty homeless people. But I'll never ever see him again, and I don't need his goddamned approval. Let him think what he thinks!' I then felt a lot better; and by the third time I tried it, I really began to feel shameless. By the fifth time, I saw the whole thing as sort of a joke, and I actually enjoyed it."

That's what frequently happens when people do REBT shame-attacking exercises. They soon feel much less uncomfortable — and sometimes downright enjoy it. In Chana's case, she soon saw that she could do shame-attacking exercises with people who knew her, as well as those who didn't; and she deliberately, at my suggestion, began telling her school friends how anxious she was about test-taking, how she kept procrastinating on her studies, how she refused to take some important subjects at school because she knew that taking then would entail taking several tests during the term. The more she confessed these weaknesses, the more she saw that most people fully accepted her with them; and she then began to accept herself. She still very much disliked her panic and her avoidances, but she put *herself* down less and less for them. Her anxiety about her anxiety appreciably decreased, and so, too, did her primary horror of test-taking. The shame-attacking exercises that she did particularly helped her to see that, on both her primary level of disturbance (panic about failing at tests) and her secondary level (horror of her original anxiety), shame was the essence of her upsetness. She saw that when she worked to reduce this shame, much of her disturbance disappeared. Her New Effective Philosophy, sparked by her shame-attacking exercise, was, "I don't need their goddamned approval. Let them think what they think!" This led her to make both a brief and *philosophically deep* change.

Skill Training

There are times where your client's problems may be compounded by a lack of skills. These skill deficits can range from actual trade skills (like using specific computer software) to interpersonal or social skills. You can encourage your clients to pursue courses and workshops on appropriate subjects to improve their skills. Pam, an administrative assistant, was very unhappy at her job and wanted to make a change professionally but was afraid of not finding anything any better. In addition to working on her demands about obtaining the "perfect" job, she also worried that her skills might be outdated. She was encouraged to explore training opportunities which might make her more marketable as an employee and eventually she attended several helpful courses. This was a practical solution — "inelegant" in a sense. Indeed, had we focused only on the training, CM probably wouldn't have been earning her keep as a therapist, but it was helpful to Pam and contributed to increasing her confidence about her professional marketability.

Often clients present with real problems in social settings. This is not to say that they are completely socially inept but that they simply have not had an opportunity to learn or practice some interpersonal skills. For example, CM has worked with many clients who presented with extreme discomfort in meeting new people. Once we had worked on decreasing their anxiety about these situations, it also became clear that some of them were not very good at initiating or maintaining conversations. This was, in most cases, not due to an intellectual deficit but more from lack of skills and practice. In these cases, we often focused on how to make small talk, how to ask open-ended questions, and ways to propose fairly non-threatening subsequent contacts when they had met people who interested them. We also find this with clients who are working on becoming more assertive instead of passive or aggressive. These clients have often been practicing their other mode of operating for so long that assertiveness skills are foreign to them. They require some coaching in regard to using "I" statements, body postures, voice volume and tone, and a variety of other areas. (Alberti & Emmons, 1995).

❖ *Paradoxical Homework*

Paradoxical homework assignments are those that, on the surface, seem to fly in the face of addressing whatever the client has come in to therapy to change. They can be cognitive, emotive, or behavioral. An insomniac may be told that he is not allowed to sleep, a person who experiences anxious thoughts may be assigned to intentionally entertain the thoughts a certain number of times a day, a compulsive masturbator can be charged with masturbating every hour on the hour, or a perfectionist may be charged with the task of making deliberate mistakes. The purpose of these types of homework assignments is to attempt to reframe your client's problems and do some reality testing in the process.

Alison had a history of generalized anxiety and was consistently afraid throughout her day that she would have anxious thoughts and, in turn, anxiety. CM's hypothesis about her was that she was mostly bringing the anxiety on herself by repeating over and over again, "I must not be anxious! I can't stand it!" We agreed to have her deliberately bring on the anxious thoughts every day for a week and see what happened. When she returned the following week, there was a remarkable change. Not only had she had difficulty getting herself anxious "on demand," but she found that she spent a great deal less time worrying about the possibility of becoming anxious. Since she was deliberately trying to get herself anxious, it seemed silly to be worried about it.

Therapists have been using paradoxical techniques with clients for many years but the approach is not without risks. It is important to keep in mind that the procedure should be used selectively and that not all clients will respond favorably. You should probably explore this option further before attempting it on your own by reading: Shohen, V., and Rohrbuagh, M. (1994). Paradoxical Intervention. In Corsini, R.I. (Ed.) *Encyclopedia of Psychology* 2nd Ed. (Vol. 3, pp 5-8) New York: Wiley.

❖ *Relapse Prevention*

Relapse prevention can include any number of cognitive, emotive/ experiential, or behavioral methods, and is usually used specifically in treating addicted clients. It is important to note that REBT takes for granted that, at the very least, most addicted clients will have impulses to relapse, so we take a proactive approach to addressing preventive techniques before it happens. We review potentially provocative thoughts and experiences which may contribute to relapse impulses, we brainstorm solutions with clients for problematic situations, and we use imagery and role playing to solidify their rational coping statements. Equally importantly, we emphasize the importance of self-acceptance if they do relapse. This is not to say that we encourage them to be O.K. with the fact that they have relapsed but we do emphasize staying away from self-downing, which will usually only contribute to further relapse. *We encourage them to condemn the act, but not themselves!*

In Vivo Desensitization

We humans often preserve our vulnerability to the things we are afraid of by systematically and religiously avoiding those things at all costs. We become so anxious and fearful of some things, and give ourselves such extreme, irrational messages about the importance of avoiding them, that every time we do manage to avoid them, we experience it as a huge relief. However, the relief stems not so much from having avoided the thing or situation but more from having avoided what we perceived to be the life threatening component of it.

Take Martie for example. She was so afraid of being the center of attention that a great deal of her daily energy was spent avoiding and manipulating situations so as to preserve anonymity. Public speaking, in her mind, was out of the question. As a section manager in a department store, she recognized that these fears were starting to negatively influence her career. Contemporaries she had started out with at the company were starting to move ahead of her in the hierarchy. She attributed this to the fact that they were better known and seemed to state their opinions and ideas more easily and readily in meetings. Having no way to know the "truth" about her co-workers, I realized that even if her assessment of others' advancement wasn't entirely accurate, at the very least she could benefit from reducing her anxiety. Through a careful assessment it became apparent that she had originally felt "nervous" about having attention focused on her and eventually that nervousness had blossomed into full blown anxiety. Interestingly, she couldn't identify ever having had a really bad experience in the limelight (many clients have and then awfulize and self-down about the experience, which increases their anxiety). Martie, on the other hand, being the intelligent woman that she was, had figured out early on that there were ways to avoid being noticed. Therefore, every time she employed one of these mechanisms and avoided notice, she not only saved herself from the attention but from her *perception of how awful and embarrassing the attention would have been had she experienced it.*

The goal of *in vivo* desensitization is to show clients that it is their irrational beliefs which are causing the extreme emotional upset, not the thing or situation they are afraid of. Through repeatedly exposing your client, either experientially or through imagery, to the thing she irrationally fears the most, you can work with her to start breaking down the strong irrationalities associated with it. She can begin to understand that, while it may continue to be uncomfortable, she can handle it and it is not nearly the threat she has created in her mind.

❖ Staying in Difficult Situations

Prescribing that your client stay in a difficult or uncomfortable situation is really a form of *in vivo* desensitization. It gives him an opportunity to work at making himself less disturbed despite being in an obnoxious situation, and then to evaluate more rationally whether it is advantageous or not to remain in the situation. It can also serve to increase his awareness that, despite being uncomfortable, he is capable of handling it.

❖ Acting on Rational Beliefs

We spend a great deal of time focused on teaching clients not to react to their irrational beliefs and, ideally, to replace them with alternative rational self-statements. Another approach involves asking your client to deliberately and mindfully push himself *to act as if he only had rational beliefs.* We also call this "behaving the way you'd like to feel." Many people make the mistake of waiting for inspiration to come before they tackle a project or make positive changes. The difficulty is that inspiration is often difficult to obtain if you're waiting around for it to strike. You, and your client, have a much better chance of experiencing some form of inspiration, or at least getting something done, if you rationally decide what's in your best interest and then make yourself act on the rational thoughts! The good news is that motivation and inspiration will sometimes follow.

In terms of implementing these interventions into your own practice, we highly recommend *The RET Resource Book For Practitioners,* edited by Michael E. Bernard, Ph.D. and Janet L. Wolfe, Ph.D. It is published by the Albert Ellis Institute and we keep a much-used copy in our staff lounge. This is a collection of extremely useful short articles, hands-on techniques, and handouts in easy to copy binder form for clients. All of the information included was submitted by longtime REBT practitioners. Topics include assertiveness training, confidence building, disputing, handling obsessive fears, overcoming procrastination, rational self-management, reducing anger, and increasing self-acceptance, to name just a few.

Some final notes on implementing any of these interventions: Homework assignments between sessions are highly emphasized in the REBT approach. Whether you assign a cognitive, emotive/experiential, or behavioral assignment, utilizing the time between your therapy sessions is equally important in facilitating your client's progress. It is vital to your success — and your clients' — that you experiment and try a variety of approaches with clients. First, it will take practice for you to comfortably integrate any new interventions into your approach. Second, just as there is evidence to suggest that individual students tend to favor a particular learning style, clients often respond especially well to certain types of interventions while others may be highly ineffectual for them. Keep an open mind, view it all as an experiment and develop your own style.

8

The Integration of REBT with Other Systems of Therapy

R EBT, as we have been showing in this book, has its own special theories and practices, but it overlaps with, and is different from, various other major systems of therapy. We shall now see how it is integrated with certain other systems.

REBT Integrated with Psychoanalytic and Psychodynamic Therapies

Psychoanalytic therapies importantly note that people have conscious as well as unconscious thoughts, feelings, and actions, that they often unawarely disturb themselves, and that they had better bring to light their unconscious motivations if they are to improve their symptoms (Freud, 1965). REBT especially agrees that clients are very often unaware of their Irrational Beliefs and, in a sense, too aware of their Rational Beliefs. However, it does not agree that clients frequently "repress" these Beliefs, and holds that most of them are just below the surface of consciousness — e.g., forgetting someone's name — and can often be quickly brought to light if clients look for them unfrantically. So a good deal of REBT consists of helping clients to find their tacit or unconscious IBs, clearly bring them to awareness, and then work at Disputing them.

REBT also partly endorses the Freudian defense system; practically all people are defensive at times in regard to acknowledging their "bad" or "wrong" behavior. Particularly when they believe that they must behave one way and they do not, they often forget, rationalize, project or otherwise defend themselves because if they acknowledged their "bad" acts they would distinctly blame themselves. Showing them that they actually behaved "badly" when they are defensive, may do more harm than good. So REBT teaches them its philosophy of unconditional acceptance (USA) and helps them to acknowledge their "bad" *deeds* but not to blame their *selves*, their *personhood*. When a client really "gets" the USA outlook, he tends to be less defensive (and especially less repressing) and keeps rating his *behavior* instead of his *self*.

REBT is closer to the *self-psychology* of Kohut (1991) than to the Freudian sexual and Oedipal theories. It sees self-denigration as central to much disturbance and especially explores self-ratings. It is in some ways closer to the *object relations* theories of Klein (1984) and Winnicott (1975) because it sees most clients as overconcerned with their human relationships rather than with other things. Moreoever, REBT helps people particularly to explore, understand, and change their Irrational Beliefs about their relationships and to acquire skill training in relating.

REBT does not usually analyze long-windedly the early childhood history of its clients, but largely focuses on their present disturbance. To help clients understand their present Irrational Beliefs, however, it often shows them how they originated in their early lives and how they have uncritically maintained them today. It also reviews how their self-defeating emotional and behavioral reactions often were established in their early lives but are actively (and sometimes unconsciously) maintained today.

For example, Maggie came to therapy because she felt "used" and "like a receptacle" when she had sexual intercourse with her husband — which she did very rarely and only when he was particularly insistent. Although they had a fairly healthy, open, and communicative relationship otherwise, the marriage was threatened by this problem. Maggie was invested in change and reported that she was very attracted to her husband. Extensive attempts at increased foreplay, non-sexual intimacy, and non-coital sexual intimacy had effected little, if any, improvement. Upon closer scrutiny, it was revealed that Maggie had been routinely sexually abused as a child by her adoptive father. At that time, she rightly believed that she was being used inappropriately by him. Unfortunately, and perhaps understandably, she carried this belief from that time forward and generalized it to all sexual contact. Thus, she believed unconsciously that all sex was "bad," "wrong," and "extremely threatening to her." She also experienced a great deal of anger at her husband for his pressure for sexual contact with her.

Here's another example. Sarah blamed her horror of criticism on the fact that her schizophrenic mother was critical of almost everything she did as a child. Therefore, she thought, she became enraged and depressed whenever anyone was critical of her today. She was hardly dissuaded from this idea even when AE showed her that her twin sister, Sally, who was also continually berated by their mother, took almost the opposite attitude and didn't take anyone's criticism too seriously. So, AE hypothesized, it couldn't have been the mother alone who made Sarah react violently to criticism. It was A, the unfair carping of the mother, *times* B, Sarah's Belief System, that made her so sensitive at C, her emotional Consequence.

Sarah didn't buy this and insisted that it was only her mother's castigation that upset her as a child and that still upset her as a thirty-year-old adult. AE helped Sarah examine what she had told herself when she was young, to make herself angry and depressed. That was easy. She clearly remembered telling herself, at that time, "It's so unfair! I'm doing everything to be a good girl and treat everybody, especially my mother, well and she keeps eagerly looking for things to blame me for and always finds them. How can she be so unfair? She's a rotten bitch! And if my own mother constantly criticizes me, without any cause, other people will also be unfair and I'll have this sort of thing all my life. How rotten people are! How depressing! People shouldn't be unfair like that!"

Sarah saw that, as a child, she strongly kept repeating these Beliefs to herself and that they, as much as anything else, contributed to her feelings of anger and depression. "A" did not by itself cause "C." A x B did.

Sarah then saw, because AE persuaded her to look for them, that she still strongly held these Beliefs today. She still believed that no one — especially her mother — *should* treat her unfairly; that if they did, *all* people would follow suit and treat her abominably; and that she couldn't be happy *at all* with this kind of criticism. It hardly occurred to her — though she had several talks with Sally who reacted with toughness to unfair treatment — that it wasn't the past or the present unfairness itself that created her upsetness, but her personal reaction to it. The more AE showed her that her childhood Beliefs were essentially the same as her thirty-year-old ideas, the more she saw that her Beliefs — not Adversities of life — were the main issue.

Sarah then began reassessing her early Beliefs, and still concluded that her mother was very unfair — as disturbed people are likely to be. But she also concluded that people *should* be unfair, when they are; that not all of them were like her mother in this respect; and that like her sister Sally, she could thoroughly dislike their unfairness, but not take it so seriously as to enrage and depress herself about it. She still shied away from her mother and from other unfair people, but she forgave her mother for being schizophrenic, and she accepted other people — but not their behavior — when they treated her unfairly.

By exploring Sarah's childhood Beliefs and getting her to think about and challenge them, AE also helped her to see how she still largely held them today, to see how irrational they were, and to stop holding them. AE used the past — which was over and once removed — to show her how she was actively continuing its ideas today, and how she could rationally Dispute them. She even carried this Disputing of her IBs into the future, took a job under a boss she knew to be highly critical, and was able to show herself in advance that his unfair criticism didn't matter that much, and meant nothing about her worth as a person. So she risked taking the job and learned to react with sorrow and frustration, but not rage and self-downing, when she worked with this difficult boss.

How REBT Is Integrated with Therapies that Emphasize Feelings

Several therapies, such as Gestalt Therapy (Perls, 1969) and Reichian (Reich, 1960) Therapy, emphasize *feeling techniques*. But so does REBT! It holds that thoughts and feelings are not disparate but intrinsically related. It points out that people have Irrational Beliefs because they start with strong desires, which they often raise to demands or musts (which themselves are cognitive-emotive). It usually begins therapy by focusing on clients' disturbed feelings (such as anxiety and depression).

REBT, as shown in chapter 6, also includes several predominantly *emotive techniques,* some of which were invented by AE and other REBT therapists. Thus, it uses shame-attacking exercises (Ellis, 1973), rational emotive imagery (Ellis, 1993;

Maultsby, 1984) and forceful coping statements and self-dialogues to help change people's thoughts and behaviors (Ellis & Velten, 1972). It also uses experiential exercises, encounter groups, marathons, and other methods that include techniques borrowed from predominantly feeling therapies (Ellis & Dryden, 1997). In fact, of the several forms of cognitive-behavior therapy now in use, REBT probably puts more emphasis on feeling techniques than do any of the other systems.

❖ *How REBT Is Integrated with Behavior Therapy*

REBT *is* behavior therapy. Behavior Therapy always included cognitive methods, especially teaching clients several behavioral techniques. But it was deficient in cognitive applications until AE began to stress the important part Irrational Beliefs played in creating disturbances and detailed specific methods of Disputing these IBs (Ellis, 1962, 1994). Over the last forty years, behavior therapy has for the most part become cognitive-behavioral, because few behavior therapists do not now use cognitions in their theory and, especially, in their practice.

REBT theory, always highly behavioral, says that strongly held Irrational Beliefs lead to dysfunctional behaviors *and* that actions (such as phobic avoidances) reinforce IBs. Just as importantly, REBT theory says that sometimes the best (and perhaps only) way to change some clients' IBs is to have them *act* against them. Thus, elevator phobics may never give up their dysfunctional Belief that elevators are very dangerous until they, many times, uncomfortably force themselves to "risk" elevator rides.

AE: "Let me say again that I probably never would have created REBT had I not overcome my own public speaking and social phobias, at the age of nineteen, when I made myself do *in vivo* desensitization many times." REBT therefore favors this form of exposure more than it favors Wolpe's (1958) imaginal method of desensitization. But REBT routinely uses a great many other behavioral methods, such as homework assignments, paradoxical homework, reinforcement, stimulus control, relapse prevention, and assertiveness training and other kinds of skill training (see chapter 7 on Behavioral Interventions). Again, REBT *is* behavior therapy — as well as one of the pioneering forms of cognitive-behavior therapy.

Radical Behavior Therapy emphasizes Skinner's theory and practice of operant conditioning but, in the form of Acceptance Therapy (Hayes, 1987), includes a number of cognitive methods. It seems to agree with REBT that a profound philosophical as well as a behavioral change is required for fundamental client improvement, but it stresses paradoxical and manipulative methods more than the cognitive restructuring methods of A. Beck (1976) and Ellis (Ellis & Dryden, 1997; Ellis, Gordon, Neenan, & Palmer, 1998). REBT, however, includes a good deal of Skinnerian operant conditioning, not to mention Pavlovian reinforcement, in its therapy procedures.

How REBT Is Integrated with Person-Centered and Existential Therapy

Carl Rogers (1957) and many other therapists with existential leanings, such as May (1969) and Yalom (1990), view individuals as having a considerable degree of choice. People are partly able to choose various patterns of thought, feeling, and action, and therefore can construct their self-helping and self-defeating behaviors. They especially go beyond other animals in choosing to have negative or positive views of their *self* or *personhood,* and take a positive or negative view of *self* or *being* and make it an important part of their functioning.

The person-centered and existentialist position, therefore, tries to help clients accept themselves unconditionally (or have what Rogers called "unconditional positive regard") just because they are alive and human, and not conditionally because they act well by themselves or with others. Then they always have self-acceptance and never have to down themselves though they can, for practical and moral purposes, definitely rate or evaluate their doings. To help clients *achieve* unconditional acceptance, person-centered and existential therapists make a point of *giving* their clients unconditional acceptance. The expectation is that if they accept the clients in spite of their failings and faults, the clients will take to this model and therefore fully accept themselves.

REBT practitioners follow this person-centered and existential model and go out of their way to give their clients unconditional acceptance because of its importance to effective human functioning. But REBT also recognizes that if the therapist merely gives acceptance, many clients may accept themselves *because* their therapist accepts them and may thus acquire highly *conditional* acceptance. REBT practitioners, therefore, in addition to giving unconditional acceptance, actively teach their clients the importance of *giving it to themselves*.

In fact, REBT teaches clients two main ways of achieving USA:

1) Choose to fully accept yourself just because you are alive and human, as every person is entitled to do. Therefore, conclude, "I am good and worthy just because I exist."

2) Refrain from giving yourself a global "rating" *at all*. Just rate your thoughts, feelings, and acts as "good" or "bad" only in regard to how they aid your goals and

values. But don't — yes, don't — rate yourself globally.
Don't rate your being, essence, or personhood.

So REBT is one of the existential psychotherapies. But
whereas most of these therapies tend to be relatively passive — as
indeed was Carl Rogers — REBT uses several active-directive
methods and hypothesizes that these make it more effective. It
actively *teaches,* as well as models, unconditional acceptance.

❖ *How REBT Is Integrated with Constructivist Therapy*

George Kelly (1955) was a pioneering constructivist therapist —
as was also Epictetus and several other ancient philosophers.
REBT is definitely a constructivist therapy, as noted in chapter 2.
A good many constructivist therapists, however, follow a
somewhat non-directive, waiting-for-their-clients-to-come-to-
their-own-conclusions procedure (Guterman, 1994). Instead,
REBT blends active-directive therapy with constructivism (Ellis,
1997). It actively teaches constructivist and existential philosophy
and encourages clients to use these in their own creative interests.

❖ *How REBT Is Integrated with Interpersonal Relationship Therapy*

Harry Stack Sullivan (1953) pioneered in helping clients to
become socially adjusted through their personal relationship with
their therapist and Klerman et al. (Klerman, G.L., Rounsville, B.,
Chevron, E., Nev, C. and Weissman, M., 1979) have emphasized
this aspect of therapy and called their system Interpersonal
Therapy (IPT). REBT has always stressed interpersonal relations
because AE was heavily into sex therapy and relationship therapy
from 1943 to 1947, before becoming a psychoanalyst:

> After I created REBT, I wrote several popular books on
> sex-love relationships (Ellis, 1957, 1958, 1960, 1976,

After I created REBT, I wrote several popular books on sex-love relationships (Ellis, 1957, 1958, 1960, 1976, 1977, 1979). In my work with clients, I emphasize several things: 1) I always do my best to accept clients unconditionally, in spite of their shortcomings and their sometimes poor behavior to me and to others. I also stress their unconditional other-acceptance (UOA). 2) Through my relationship with them I examine their relationships with others — though at times this may be difficult — to ascertain and hopefully correct their ineffective social relations. 3) I similarly focus on their interpersonal relations with others and sometimes give them skill training in social relating. 4) I sometimes place them in one of my therapy groups, to further examine how they relate to other group members and to give them practice working on their social skills. 5) I recommend workshops, lectures, books, and audio-visual materials to help clients be more socially effective.

In many ways, then, through individual relationships with the therapist as well as group and other procedures REBT focuses on helping people with their interpersonal relationships.

❖ *How REBT Is Integrated with Family Systems Therapy*

Family systems therapy has many aspects but in general it holds that individuals in a family are importantly affected by the family system, that this has to be taken into account in treating them, and that manipulating the system is often an effective method of helping the individuals in the family. REBT largely agrees with these propositions. But it adds to systems therapy the element of treating family members for their own individual disturbances as well as treating them by systemic methods.

Joan was angry at her husband, Dan, because he "inconsiderately" demanded sex with her at least twice a week when she usually wanted it about once a month. Dan was angry at Joan, in turn, for depriving him of the sex he "needed" and was also depressed because he thought that he supposedly wasn't attractive enough for Joan. Using REBT, AE showed Joan her Irrational Beliefs leading to her anger: namely, "Dan *must* not keep after me for sex when he knows I am not as arousable as he is. He's an *inconsiderate* person and I *can't stand* him!" When Joan acknowledged these IBs, and Disputed them, she came up with some Rational Beliefs and an Effective New Philosophy: "I *wish* Dan were more considerate, but he doesn't *have to* be. He acts inconsiderately at times but at other times he acts quite kindly and considerately and therefore is not an *inconsiderate person*. I don't like some of his behaviors but I *can* stand him and even love him."

Dan was helped to see his own Irrational Beliefs, which were: "I *need* sex at least twice a week. It's *awful* to have Joan depriving me of what I *need*. As my wife, she *absolutely shouldn't* frustrate me. What a sexless bitch she is!" Dan disputed these IBs and changed them to rational preferences: "I *prefer* sex at least twice a week, but I don't *need* it. I won't die without it. I can see that it's really against my interests but not *awful,* not *totally bad*. If Joan is as sexless as I think she is, she *should be* that sexless and is not a bitch. Let me see if I can drop my rage and have a better chance to convince her to have more sex. Meanwhile, even if I'm not that attractive to her, I need not put my entire self down and depress myself."

Joan and Dan changed their disturbed thinking and changed their unhealthy anger at each other into feelings of healthy disappointment and regret. Dan stopped his self-downing and depression. They were then much more ready to change their marital system. Usually, system changing is put off somewhat because if family members are still angry, depressed, or hostile, (as some of them may well be in almost any kind of system), and if the therapist helps them by suggesting sensible changes in the system, there is a good chance that they will louse up the new system. If they are first helped to change their self-disturbing tendencies — which perhaps almost all humans are prone to have in all systems — then they often can, with and without help, change the system.

Actually, AE suggested several system changes which Joan and Dan were able to experiment with and which helped their family situation: First, both could try to view sex as "sex play" and not as "intercourse." Then Joan could satisfy Dan with her fingers or tongue two or three times a week, while he satisfied her with intercourse twice a month. Second, Dan could please Joan in several nonsexual ways — such as doing more of the shopping, house cleaning, and cooking — so that she would see him as being "more considerate." Third, Dan could also reinforce Joan for going out of her way to satisfy him sexually; either coitally or noncoitally, by being especially attentive to her. She particularly appreciated fresh flowers, so when she was sexually cooperative he gratefully supplied them. These and other changes in the family system — some of which the couple came up with themselves — worked fairly well. So this use of REBT with both Joan and Dan individually, as well as arranging some changes in the system, worked reciprocally and probably better than the use of individual or family system therapy by itself.

How REBT Is Integrated with Other Cognitive Behavior Therapies

REBT in 1955 was the first of the modern cognitive behavior therapies and was followed, a decade later, by several other therapies, especially those of Beck (1976) and Meichenbaum

(1977). Most of them used REBT's methods of Disputing clients' Irrational Beliefs or similar cognitive restructuring, and to this day they still do. Therefore, REBT is importantly close to and integrated with them.

Beck's Cognitive Therapy (A. Beck, 1976; J. Beck, 1993) is more similar to REBT than are several other cognitive behavior therapies. At first, cognitive therapy stressed the Disputing of clients' "automatic thoughts" rather than their core IBs; more recently it has emphasized REBT's restructuring of core beliefs, especially with clients who have severe personality disorders. However, where REBT considers *musts* and *demands* basic to most IBs, Cognitive Therapy puts them on an equal footing with *dysfunctional automatic thoughts,* such as personalizing. A. Beck (1976) originally omitted REBT's emphasis on strong emotional and exposure techniques of therapy but in recent years cognitive therapists have moved closer to REBT in this respect (J. Beck, 1993).

The constructivist cognitive behavior therapies, such as those of Guidano (1991), Kelly (1955), Mahoney (1991), and the Neimeyers (Neimeyer & Mahoney, 1995), use a similar theory to REBT, in that they emphasize clients' innate tendencies to change their dysfunctional thoughts, feelings, and behaviors. These approaches tend to be less active-directive than REBT, however, and less likely to use highly emotive-evocative and *in vivo* desensitization methods. Research studies of how effective they are, compared to REBT (Ellis & Dryden, 1997; Ellis, Gordon, Neenan, & Palmer, 1978) and CT (A. Beck, 1976; A. Beck & G. Emery, 1985; J. Beck, 1993) may provide important findings about which systems of therapy work better with what kinds of clients.

Summary

While the basic philosophy and principles of REBT have remained consistent, the practice of REBT continues to evolve. What we have attempted to give you with this book is not only an overview of the theory but the most current information about the practice and specific interventions used at the Institute in New York and by REBT practitioners all over the world.

We certainly do not claim to have created all of the interventions which we use. As mentioned throughout the book, we have borrowed some excellent methods from a variety of sources — as with any adaptive, flexible model — and we encourage you to do the same in your own practice.

Here are some of the most important final points to remember:

- Use your own style! There is very little which is less therapeutic than a practitioner who uncomfortably attempts to practice in a way which doesn't fit his or her personality. One of the practical aspects of this approach is that it can be integrated into just about anyone's style. If the way you are implementing it feels really uncomfortable to you, it won't work until you add more of your "genuine" self to the mix!

- The assessment phase is vital and an ongoing process! Clients may often test you at the beginning of therapy with a "test" problem to see how you handle it and it's your job to prove that you are equal to the task!

- Use REBT on yourself! One of the best ways to become familiar with the theory and with yourself is to apply the principles to your own life and figure out what your own irrational thinking entails. If you don't know what your buttons are, it's going to be more difficult for you to help a client identify hers!

- Practice, Practice, Practice! Be mindful of the fact that different people respond to different interventions. The better a repertoire you have to work with, the more success you will enjoy with a variety of clients!

Appendix A:
How to Maintain and Enhance Your Rational Emotive Behavior Therapy Gains

— Albert Ellis, Ph.D.

If you work at using the principles and practices of Rational Emotive Behavior Therapy (REBT), you will be able to change your self-defeating thoughts, feelings, and behaviors and to feel much better than when you started therapy. Good! But you will also, at times, fall back — and sometimes far back. No one is perfect and practically all people take one step backward to every two or three steps forward. Why? Because that is the nature of humans: to improve, to stop improving at times, and sometimes to backslide.

How can you (imperfectly!) slow down your tendency to fall back? How can you maintain and enhance your therapy goals? Here are some methods that we have tested at our Institute's clinic in New York and that many of our clients have found effective.

How to Maintain Your Improvement

1. When you improve and then fall back to old feelings of anxiety, depression, or self-downing, try to remind yourself and pinpoint exactly what thoughts, feelings, and behaviors you once changed

123

to bring about your improvement. If you again feel depressed, think back to how you previously used REBT to make yourself undepressed. For example, you may remember that:

a. You stopped telling yourself that you were worthless and that you couldn't ever succeed in getting what you wanted.

b. You did well in a job or a love affair and proved to yourself that you did have some ability and that you were lovable.

c. You forced yourself to go on interviews instead of avoiding them and thereby helped yourself overcome your anxiety about them.

Remind yourself of past thoughts, feelings, and behaviors that you have helped yourself by changing.

2. Keep thinking, thinking, and thinking Rational Beliefs (RBs) or coping statements, such as: "It's great to succeed but I can fully accept myself as a person and have enjoyable experiences even when I fail!" Don't merely parrot these statements but go over them carefully many times and think them through until you really begin to believe and feel that they are true.

3. Keep seeking for, discovering, and disputing and challenging your Irrational Beliefs (IBs) with which you are once again upsetting yourself. Take each important Irrational Belief — such as, "I have to succeed in order to be a worthwhile person!" — and keep asking yourself: "Why is this belief true?" "Where is the evidence that my worth to myself, and my enjoyment of living, utterly depends on my succeeding at something?" "How does failing at an important task make me totally unacceptable as a human?"

Keep forcefully and persistently disputing your Irrational Beliefs whenever you see that you are letting them creep back again. And even when you don't actively hold them, realize that they may arise once more, bring them to your consciousness, and preventively — and vigorously! — dispute them.

4. Keep risking and doing things that you irrationally fear — such as riding in elevators, socializing, job hunting, or creative writing. Once you have partly overcome one of your irrational fears, keep acting against it on a regular basis. If you feel uncomfortable in forcing yourself to do things that you are unrealistically afraid of doing, don't allow yourself to avoid doing them — or else you'll preserve your discomfort forever! Practice making yourself as uncomfortable as you can be, in order to eradicate your irrational fears and to become unanxious and comfortable later.

5. Try to clearly see the real difference between *healthy* negative feelings — such as those of sorrow, regret, and frustration, when you do not get some of the important things you want — and *unhealthy* negative feelings, such as depression, anxiety, self-hatred, and self-pity.

Whenever you feel *over*concerned (panicked) or *unduly* miserable (depressed) acknowledge that you are having a statistically normal but a psychologically unhealthy feeling and that you are mainly bringing it on yourself with some dogmatic *should, ought,* or *must.*

Realize that you are capable of changing your unhealthy (or *mustur*batory) feelings back into appropriate (or preferential) ones. Take your depressed feelings and work on them until you only feel sorry and regretful. Take your anxious feelings and work on them until you only feel concerned and apprehensive. Use rational emotive imagery to vividly imagine unpleasant Activating Events even before they happen; let yourself feel unhealthily upset (anxious, depressed, enraged, or self-downing) as you imagine them; then work on your feelings to change them to healthy negative emotions (concern, sorrow, annoyance, or regret) as you keep imagining some of the worst things happening. Don't give up until you actually do change your feelings.

6. Avoid self-defeating procrastination. Do unpleasant tasks fast — today! If you still procrastinate, reward yourself with certain things that you enjoy — for example, eating, vacationing, reading, and socializing — only *after* you have performed the tasks that you easily avoid. If this won't work, give yourself a severe penalty — such as talking to a boring person for two hours or burning a hundred dollar bill — every time you procrastinate.

7. Show yourself that it is an absorbing *challenge* and something of an *adventure* to maintain your emotional health and to keep yourself reasonably happy no matter what kind of misfortunes assail you. Make the uprooting of your misery one of the most important things in your life — something you are utterly determined to steadily work at achieving. Fully acknowledge that you almost always have some choice about how to think, feel, and behave; then throw yourself actively into making that choice for yourself.

8. Remember — and use — the three main insights of REBT that were first outlined in *Reason and Emotion in Psychotherapy* in 1962:

Insight No. 1: You largely *choose* to disturb yourself about the unpleasant events of your life, although you may be encouraged to do so by external happenings and by social learning. You mainly *feel the way you think.* When obnoxious and frustrating things happen to you at point A (Activating Events or Adversities), you consciously or unconsciously *select* Rational Beliefs (RBs) that lead you to feel sad and regretful and you also *select* Irrational Beliefs (IBs) that lead you to feel anxious, depressed, and self-hating.

Insight No. 2: No matter how or when you acquired your Irrational Beliefs and your self-sabotaging habits, you now, in the present, *choose* to maintain them — and that is why you are *now* disturbed. Your past history and your present life conditions importantly *affect* you; but they don't *disturb* you. Your present *philosophy* is the main contributor to your *current* disturbance.

Insight No. 3: There is no magical way for you to change your personality and your strong tendencies to needlessly upset yourself. Basic personality change requires persistent *work and practice* — yes, *work and practice* — to enable you to alter your Irrational Beliefs, your unhealthy feelings, and your self-destructive behaviors.

9. Steadily and unfrantically look for personal pleasure and enjoyments — such as reading, entertainment, sports, hobbies, art, science, and other vital absorbing interests. Make your major life goal not only the achievement of emotional health but also that of real enjoyment. Try to become involved in a long-term purpose, goal, or interest in which you can remain truly absorbed. A good happy life will give you something to live for; will distract you from many serious woes; and will encourage you to preserve and to improve your mental health.

10. Try to keep in touch with several other people who know something about REBT and who can help you get over some of its aspects with you. Tell them about problems that you have difficulty coping with and let them know how you are using REBT to overcome these problems. See if they agree with your solutions and can suggest additional and better kinds of REBT disputing that you can use to work against your Irrational Beliefs.

11. Practice suing REBT with some of your friends, relatives, and associates who are willing to let you try to help them with it.

The more often you use it with others, and are able to see what their IBs are and to try to talk them out of these self-defeating ideas, the more you will be able to understand the main principles of REBT and to use them with yourself. When you see other people act irrationally and in a disturbed manner, try to figure out — with or without talking to them about it — what their main Irrational Beliefs probably are and how these could be actively and vigorously disputed.

12. When you are in REBT individual or group therapy, try to tape record many of your sessions and listen to these carefully between sessions, so that some of the ideas that you learned in therapy sink in. After therapy has ended, play these tape recordings back to yourself from time to time to remind you how to deal with some of your old problems or new ones that may arise.

❖ *How to Deal with Backsliding*

1. Accept your backsliding as normal — as something that happens to almost all people who at first improve emotionally and who then fall back. See it as part of your human fallibility. Don't make yourself feel ashamed when some of your old symptoms return; and don't think that you have to handle them entirely by yourself and that it is wrong or weak for you to seek some additional sessions of therapy and to talk to your friends about your renewed problems.

2. When you backslide, look at your self-defeating *behavior* as bad and unfortunate; but refuse to put *yourself* down for engaging in this behavior. Use the highly important REBT principle of refraining from rating *you*, your *self*, or your *being* but of measuring only your *acts*, *deeds*, and *traits*. You are always a *person who* acts well or badly — and never a *good person* nor a *bad person*. No matter how badly you fall back and bring on your old

disturbances again, work at fully accepting yourself *with* this unfortunate or weak behavior — and then try, and keep trying, to change your behavior.

3. Go back to the ABCs of REBT and clearly see what you did to fall back to your old symptoms. At A(Activating Events or Adversity), you usually experienced some failure or rejection. At RB (Rational Belief) you probably told yourself that you didn't *like* failing and didn't *want* to be rejected. If you only stayed with these Rational Beliefs, you would merely feel sorry, regretful, disappointed, or frustrated. But if you felt disturbed, you probably then went on to some Irrational Beliefs (IBs), such as: "I *must* not fail! It's *horrible* when I do!" "I *have to* be accepted, because if I'm not that makes me an *unlovable worthless person!*" If you reverted to these IBs, you probably felt, at C (emotional Consequence) once again depressed and self-downing.

4. When you find your Irrational Beliefs by which you are once again disturbing yourself, just as you originally used Disputing (D) to challenge and surrender them, do so again — *immediately* and *persistently*. Thus, you can ask yourself, "Why *must* I not fail? Is it really *horrible* if I do?" And you can answer: "There is no reason why I *must* not fail, though I can think of several reasons why it would be highly undesirable. It's not *horrible* if I do fail — only distinctly *inconvenient*.

You can also Dispute your other Irrational Beliefs by asking yourself, "Where is it written that I *have* to be accepted? How do I become an *unlovable, worthless person* if I am rejected?" And you can answer: "I never *have to be* accepted, though I would very much *prefer* to be. If I am rejected, that makes me, alas, a *person who* is rejected this time by this individual under these conditions, but it hardly makes me an *unlovable, worthless person* who will always be rejected by anyone for whom I really care."

5. Keep looking for, finding, and actively and vigorously Disputing your Irrational Beliefs to which you have once again relapsed and that are now making you feel anxious or depressed. Keep doing this, over and over, until you build intellectual and emotional muscle (just as you would build physical muscle by learning how to exercise and then by *continuing* to exercise).

6. Don't fool yourself into believing that if you merely change your language you will always change your thinking. If you neurotically tell yourself, "I *must* succeed and be approved and you change this self-statement to "I *prefer* to succeed and be approved, you may still really be convinced, "But I really *have to* do well to be loved." Before you stop your Disputing and before you are satisfied with your answers to it, keep on doing it until you are *really* convinced of your rational answers and until your feelings of disturbance truly disappear. Then do the same thing many, many times — until your new E (Effective Philosophy) becomes hardened and habitual — which it almost always will if you keep working at arriving at it and thinking it through.

7. Convincing yourself lightly or "intellectually" of your new Effective Philosophy or Rational Beliefs often won't help very much or persist very long. Do so very *strongly* and *vigorously,* and do so many times. Thus, you can *powerfully* convince yourself, until you really *feel* it: "I no not *need* what I *want!*" "I never *have* to succeed, no matter how great I *wish* to do so!" "I *can* stand being rejected by someone I care for. It won't *kill* me — and I *still* can lead a happy life!" "No human is damnable and worthless — including and especially *me!*"

How to Generalize from Working on One Emotional Problem to Working on Other Problems

1. Show yourself that your present emotional problem and the ways in which you bring it on are not unique and that most

emotional and behavioral difficulties are largely created by Irrational Beliefs (IBs). Whatever your IBs are, you can overcome them by strongly and persistently disputing and acting against them.

2. Recognize that you tend to have three major kinds of Irrational Beliefs that lead you to disturb yourself and that the emotional and behavioral problems that you want to relieve fall into one, two, or all three of these categories:

a. "I *must* do well and *have to* be approved by people whom I find important." This IB leads you to feel anxious, depressed, and self-hating; and to avoid doing things at which you may fail or avoiding relationships that may not turn out well.

b. "Other people *must* treat me fairly and nicely!" This IB contributes to your feeling angry, furious, violent, and over-rebellious.

c. "The conditions under which I live *must* be comfortable and free from major hassles!" This IB tends to bring about feelings of low frustration tolerance and self-pity; and sometimes those of anger and depression.

3. Recognize that when you employ one of these three absolutistic *musts* — or any of the innumerable variations on it — you naturally and commonly derive from them other irrational conclusions, such as:

a. "Because I am not doing as well as I *must,* I am an incompetent worthless individual!" (Self-downing).

b. "Since I am not being approved by people whom I find important, as I *have to* be, it's *awful* and *terrible!*" (Awfulizing).

c. "Because others are not treating me as fairly and as nicely as they *absolutely should* treat me, they are *utterly rotten people* and deserve to be damned!" (Damnation).

d. "Since the conditions under which I live are not that comfortable and since my life has several major hassles, as it *must* not have, I can't stand it! My existence is a horror!" (Can't-stand-it-itis).

e. "Because I have failed and gotten rejected as I absolutely *ought not* have done, I'll *always* fail and *never* get accepted as I *must* be! My life will be hopeless and joyless forever!" (Overgeneralizing).

4. Work at seeing that these Irrational Beliefs are part of your *general* repertoire of thoughts and feelings and that you bring them to many different kinds of situations. Realize that in most cases where you feel seriously upset and act in a self-defeating manner you are consciously or unconsciously sneaking in one or more of these IBs. Consequently, if you reduce them in one area and are still emotionally disturbed about something else, you can use the same REBT principles to discover your IBs in the new area and to minimize them there.

5. Repeatedly show yourself that you normally won't disturb yourself and remain disturbed if you abandon your absolutistic *shoulds, oughts,* and *musts* and consistently replace them with flexible and unrigid (though still strong) *desires* and *preferences.*

6. Continue to acknowledge that you can change your Irrational Beliefs (IBs) by rigorously (not rigidly!) using realistic and healthy thinking. You can show yourself that your Irrational Beliefs are only assumptions or hypotheses — not facts. You can logically, realistically, and pragmatically dispute them in many ways such as these:

a. You can show yourself that your IBs are self-defeating — that they interfere with your goals and your happiness. For if you firmly convince yourself, "I *must* succeed at important tasks and *have to* be approved by all the significant people in my life," you will of course at times fail and be disapproved — and thereby inevitably make yourself anxious and depressed instead of sorry and frustrated.

b. Your Irrational Beliefs do not conform to reality — and especially do not conform to the facts of human fallibility. If you always *had* to succeed, if the universe commanded that you *must* do so, you obviously *would* always succeed. But of course you often don't! If you invariably *had* to be approved by others, you could never be disapproved. But obviously you frequently are! The universe is clearly not arranged so that you will always get what you demand. So although your desires are often realistic, your godlike commands definitely are not.

c. Your Irrational Beliefs are illogical, inconsistent, or contradictory. No matter how much you *want* to succeed and to be approved, it never follows that therefore you *must* do well in these (or any other) respects. No matter how desirable justice or politeness is, it never *has to* exist.

Although REBT disputing is not infallible or sacred, it efficiently helps you to discover which of your beliefs are irrational and self-defeating and how to use realistic pragmatic, and logical thinking to minimize them. If you keep using flexible thinking, you will avoid dogma and set up your assumptions about you, other people, and world conditions so that you always keep them open to change.

7. Try to set up some main goals and purposes in life — goals that you would like very much to reach but that you never tell yourself that you absolutely must attain. Keep checking to see how you are coming along with these goals, and at times revise them. Keep yourself oriented toward the goals that you select and that are not harmful to you or to others. Instead of making yourself extremely self-interested or socially-interested, a balanced absorption in both these kinds of goals will often work out best for you and the community in which you choose to live.

8. If you get bogged down and begin to lead a life that seems too miserable or dull, review the points made here and work at using them. If you fall back or fail to go forward at the pace you prefer, don't hesitate to return to therapy for some booster sessions.

Author's note:

I gratefully acknowledge the contribution of the following people at the Institute for Rational-Emotive Therapy in New York who read this pamphlet when it was in manuscript and who made valuable comments on it: Raymond DiGuiseppe, Mal Holland, Terry Jordan, Leonor Lega, Naomi McCormick, Harriet Mischel, Beverly Pieren, Susan Presby, Karin Schleider, Janet Wolfe, Joe Yankura, and Thea Zeeve. However, I take all responsibility for the views expressed.

Reprinted with permission from a pamphlet published by The Institue for Rational-Emotive Therapy, New York.

Appendix B:
References/Resources

Note: The references which are referred to in the text are in boldface type. The items preceded by an asterisk (*) in the following list are recommended for those of you who would like more details about Rational Emotive Behavior Therapy (REBT) and Cognitive Behavior Therapy (CBT). Those preceded by two asterisks (**) are REBT and CBT self-help books and materials. Many of these publications can be obtained from the Albert Ellis Institute, 45 East 65th Street, New York, NY 10021-6593. The Institute's free catalogue and the materials it distributes may be ordered on weekdays by phone (212-535-0822) or by FAX (212-249-3582). The Institute will continue to make available these and other materials, and it will offer talks, workshops, and training sessions, as well as other presentations in the area of human growth and healthy living, and list these in its regular free catalogue. The Institute also offers corporate consulting and training. Several of the references listed here are not referred to in the text, especially a number of the self-help materials.

*Abrams, M., & Ellis, A. (1994). Rational emotive behavior therapy in the treatment of stress. *British Journal of Guidance and Counseling, 22,* 39-50.

**Adler, A. (1927). *Understanding human nature.* Garden City, NY: Greenberg.

Adler, A. (1929). *The science of living.* New York: Greenberg.

**Adler, A. (1958). *What life should mean to you.* New York: Capricorn.

*Adler, A. (1964a). *Social interest: A challenge to mankind.* New York: Capricorn.

*Adler, A. (1964b). *Superiority and social interest.* Ed. by H. L. Ansbacker & R. R. Ansbacker. Evanston, IL: Northwestern University Press.

Alberti, R.E., & Emmons, M.L. (1995) *Your perfect right,* 7th rev. ed. San Luis Obispo, CA: Impact Publishers, Inc.

*Ansbacher, H. L., & Ansbacher, R. (1956). *The individual psychology of Alfred Adler.* New York: Basic Books.

*Assaglioli, R. A. (1956). *Psychosynthesis.* New York: Hobbs-Dorman.

*Baisden, H. E. (1980). *Irrational beliefs: A construct validation study.* Unpublished doctoral dissertation. University of Minnesota, Minneapolis.

**Baldon, A., & Ellis, A. (1993). *RET problem solving workbook.* New York: Institute for Rational-Emotive Therapy.

*Bandura, A. (1986). *Social foundations of thought and action: A social cognitive theory.* Englewood Cliffs, NJ: Prentice-Hall.

Bandura, A. (1997). *Self-efficacy: the exercise of control.* New York: Freeman.

*Barlow, D. H. (1989). *Anxiety and its disorders: The nature and treatment of anxiety and panic.* New York: Guilford.

**Barlow, D. H., & Craske, M. G. (1989). *Mastery of your anxiety and panic.* Albany, NY: Center for Stress and Anxiety Disorders.

Bartley, W. W., III. (1984). *The retreat to commitment,* rev. ed. Peru, IL: Open Court.

*Bard, J. (1980). *Rational-emotive therapy in practice.* Champaign, IL: Research Press.

Beck, A. T. (1976). *Cognitive therapy and the emotional disorders.* New York: International Universities Press.

**Beck, A. T. (1988). *Love is not enough.* New York: Harper & Row.

*Beck, A. T. (1991). Cognitive therapy: A 30-year retrospective. *American psychologist, 46,* 382-389.

Beck, A. T., & Emery, G. (1985). *Anxiety disorders and phobias.* New York: Basic Books.

*Beck, A. T., Freeman, A., & Associates. (1990). *Cognitive therapy of personality disorders.* New York: Guilford.

*Beck, A. T., Rush, A. J., Shaw, B. F., & Emery, G. (1979). *Cognitive therapy of depression.* New York: Guilford.

Beck, J.S. (1995). *Cognitive therapy and beyond.* New York: Guilford.

Beckfield, D. (1998). *Master your panic and take back your life!* San Luis Obispo, CA: Impact Publishers, Inc.

**Benson, H. (1975). *The relaxation response.*New York: Morrow.

*Berkowitz, L. (1990). On the formation and regulation of anger and aggression. *American Psychologist. 45,* 494-503.

Bernard, M. E., ed. (1991). *Using rational-emotive therapy effectively: A practitioner's guide.* New York: Plenum.

**Bernard, M. E. (1993). *Staying rational in an irrational world.* New York: Carol Publishing.

*Bernard, M. E., & DiGiuseppe, R., eds. (1989). *Inside RET: A critical appraisal of the theory and therapy of Albert Ellis.* San Diego, CA: Academic Press.

*Bernard, M. E., & Joyce, M. R. (1995). *Rational-emotive therapy with children and adolescents,* 2nd ed. New York: Wiley.

Bernard, M. E., & Wolfe, J. L., eds. (1993). *The RET resource book for practitioners.* New York: Institute for Rational-Emotive Therapy.

*Bernheim, H. (1947). *Suggestive therapeutics.* New York: London Book Company. (Original publication, 1986).

*Beutler, L.E., Engle, D., Mohr, D., Daldrup, R. J., Bergan, J., Meredith, K., & Merry, W. (1991). Predictors of differential response to cognitive, experiential and self-directed therapeutic procedures. *Journal of Consulting and Clinical Psychology, 59,* 333-340.

*Blatt, S. J., & Felsen, I. (1993). Different kinds of folks may need different kinds of strokes. *Psychotherapy Research, 3,* 245-259.

*Blau, S. F. (1993). Cognitive darwinism: rational-emotive therapy and the theory of neuronal group selection. *ETC: A Review of General Semantics, 50,* 403-441.

**Bloomfield, H. H., & McWilliams, P. (1994). *How to heal depression.* Los Angeles: Prelude Press.

*Bricault, L. (1992). "Cherchex le 'should'! Cherchez le 'must'! Une entrevue avec Albert Ellis, l'initiateur de la méthode émotivo-rationelle." *Confrontation, 14,*3-12.

**Broder, M. S. (1990). *The art of living.* New York: Avon.

**Broder, M. S. (1994). *The art of staying together.* New York: Avon.

*Brown, G., & Beck, A. T. (1989). The role of imperatives in psychopathology: A reply to Ellis. *Cognitive Therapy and Research, 13,* 315-321.

*Budman, S. H., & Gurman, A. S. (1988). *Theory and practice of brief therapy.* New York: Guilford.

*Budman, S. H., Hoyt, M. F., & Friedman, S., eds. (1992). *The first session in brief therapy.* New York: Guilford.

**Burns, D. D. (1980). *Feeling good: The new mood therapy.* New York: Morrow.

**Burns, D. (1984). *Intimate connections.* New York: Morrow.

**Burns, D. D. (1989). *Feeling good handbook.* New York: Morrow.

**Burns, D. D. (1993). *Ten days to self-esteem.* New York: Morrow.

*Cade, B., & O'Hanlon, W. H. (1993). *A brief guide to brief therapy.* New York: Norton.

*Carlson, C. R., & Hoyle, R. H. (1993). Efficacy of abbreviated progressive muscle relaxation training: A quantitative review of behavioral medicine research. *Journal of Consulting and Clinical Psychology, 61,* 1059-1067.

*Clark, D.A. (1997). Twenty years of cognitive assessment: current status and future directions. *Journal of Consulting and Clinical Psychology, 65,* 996-1000.

*Cloitre, M. (1993, Winter). An interview with Martin Seligman. *Behavior Therapist,* pp. 261-263.

*Cocker, K. I., Bell, D. R., & Kidman, A. D. Cognitive behavior therapy with advanced breast cancer. *Psycho-oncology, 3,* 233-237.

*Cohen, E. D. (1992). Syllogizing RET: Applying formal logic in rational-emotive therapy. *Journal of Rational-Emotive and Cognitive Behavior Therapy, 10,* 235-252.

*Corey, G. (1994). *Theory and practice of counseling and psychotherapy,* 5th ed. Pacific Grove, CA: Brooks/Cole.

*Corsini, R. J. (1979). The betting technique. *Individual Psychology, 16,* 5-11.

*Corsini, R. J., & Wedding, D. (1995)., *Current psychotherapies.* Itasca, IL: Peacock.

*Coté, G., Gautier, J. G., Laberge, B., Cormier, H. J., & Plamondon, J. (1994). Reduced therapist contact in the cognitive behavioral treatment of panic disorder. *Behavior Therapy, 25,* 123-145.

**Coué, E. (1923). *My method.* New York: Doubleday, Page.

*Cramer, D., & Ellis, A. (1988). Irrational beliefs and strength in appropriateness of feelings: A debate. In W. Dryden & P. Trower, eds. *Developments in rational-emotive therapy* (pp.56-64). Philadelphia: Open University.

**Crawford, T. (1988). *The five coordinates for a good relationship and better communication.* Santa Barbara, CA: Author.

**Crawford, T. (1993). *Changing a frog into a prince or princess.* Santa Barbara, CA: Author.

*Crawford, T., & Ellis, A. (1982, October). Communication and rational-emotive therapy. Workshop presented in Los Angeles.

*Crawford, T., & Ellis, A. (1989). A dictionary of rational-emotive feelings and behaviors. *Journal of Rational-Emotive and Cognitive-Behavioral Therapy, 7*(1), 3-27. Developments in rational-emotive therapy (pp.56-64). Philadelphia: Open University.

**Csikszentmihalyi, M. (1990). *Flow: The psychology of optimal experience.* San Francisco: Harper Perennial.

*Cummings, N. (1994, February) Comments on programmed material and psychotherapy. *Assembly of the 21st Century.* American Psychological Association, Washington, DC.

*Cuon, D. W. (1994). Cognitive-behavioral interventions with avoidant personality: A single case study. *Journal of Cognitive Psychotherapy, 8,* 243-257.

*Curry, S. J. (1993). Self-help interventions for smoking cessation. *Journal of Consulting and Clinical Psychology, 61,* 790-803.

**Danysh, J. (1974). *Stop without quitting.* San Francisco: International Society for General Semantics.

**DeBono, E. (1991). *I am right. You are wrong: From rock logic to water logic.* New York: Viking.

*Dengelegi, L. (1990, April 25). Don't judge yourself. New York Times, p.C3.

Derrida, J. (1976). *Of grammatology.* Baltimore, MD: Johns Hopkins University.

*deShazer, S. (1985). *Keys to solution in brief therapy.* New York: Norton.

*deShazer, S. (1990). Brief therapy. In J. K. Zeig & W. M. Munion, eds. *What is psychotherapy?* (pp.278-282). San Francisco: Jossey-Bass.

*DiGiuseppe, R. (1986). The implication of the philosophy of science for rational-emotive theory and therapy. *Psychotherapy, 23,*634-639.

**DiGiuseppe, R., speaker. (1990). *What do I do with my anger: Hold it in or let it out?* Cassette recording. New York: Institute for Rational-Emotive Therapy.

*DiGiuseppe, R. (1991a). Comprehensive cognitive disputing in RET. In M. E. Bernard, ed., *Using rational-emotive therapy effectively,* pp. 173-196. New York: Plenum.

**DiGiuseppe, R., speaker. (1991b). *Maximizing the moment: How to have more fun and happiness in life.* Cassette recording. New York: Institute for Rational-Emotive Therapy.

*DiGiuseppe, R., Leaf, R., & Linscott, J. (1993). The therapeutic relationship in rational-emotive therapy: A preliminary analysis. *Journal of Rational-Emotive and Cognitive Behavior Therapy, 11,* 223-233.

*DiGiuseppe, R. A., Miller, N. J., & Trexler, L. D. (1979). A review of rational-emotive psychotherapy outcome studies. In A. Ellis & J. M. Whiteley, eds, *Theoretical and empirical foundations of rational-emotive therapy* (pp.218-235). Monterey, CA: Brooks/Cole.

*DiGiuseppe, R., Tafrate, R., & Eckhardt, C. (1994). Critical issues in the treatment of anger. *Cognitive and Behavioral Practice, 1,* 111-132.

*DiMattia, D., & Lega, L., eds. (1990). *Will the real Albert Ellis please stand up? Anecdotes by his colleagues, students and friends celebrating his 75th birthday.* New York: Institute for Rational-Emotive Therapy.

**DiMattia, D. J. & others, speakers. (1987). *Mind over myths: Handling difficult situations in the workplace.* Cassette recording. New York: Institute for Rational-Emotive Therapy.

Dobson, K. S. (1989). A meta-analysis of the efficacy of cognitive therapy for depression. *Journal of Consulting and Clinical Psychology, 57,* 414-419.

*Dougher, M. J. (1993). On the advantages and implications of a radical behavioral treatment of private events. *The Behavior Therapist, 16,* 204-206.

*Dougher, M. J. (1994). More on the differences between radical behavioral and rational emotive approaches to acceptance: A response to Robb. *Behavior Therapist.*

*Dryden, W. (1987). Language and meaning in rational-emotive therapy. In W. Dryden, ed. *Current issues in rational-emotive therapy.* London: Croom Helm.

*Dryden, W. (1990). *Dealing with anger problems: Rational-Emotive therapeutic interventions.* Sarasota, FL: Professional Resource Exchange.

Dryden, W. (1994a). *Progress in rational emotive behavior therapy.* London: Whurr.

*Dryden, W. (1994b). *Invitation to rational-emotive psychology.* London: Whurr.

**Dryden, W. (1994c). *Overcoming guilt!* London: Sheldon.

*Dryden, W., Backx, W., & Ellis, A. (1987). Problems in living: The Friday Night Workshop. In W. Dryden, *Current issues in rational-emotive therapy.* (pp.154-170). London and New York: Croom Helm.

*Dryden, W., & DiGiuseppe, R. (1990). *A primer on rational-emotive therapy.* Champaign, IL: Research Press.

*Dryden, W., & Ellis, A. (1989). Albert Ellis: An efficient and passionate life. *Journal of Counseling and Development, 67,* 539-546. Reprinted: New York: Institute for Rational-Emotive Therapy.

**Dryden, W. & Gordon, J. (1991). *Think your way to happiness.* London: Sheldon Press.

**Dryden, W., & Gordon, J. (1993). *Peak performance.* Oxfordshire, England: Mercury.

*Dryden, W. & Hill, L. K., eds. (1993). *Innovations in rational-emotive therapy.* Newbury Park, CA: Sage.

*Dryden, W., & Neenan, M. (1995). *Dictionary of rational emotive behavior therapy.* London: Whurr Publishers.

*Dryden, W. & Yankura, J. (1992). *Daring to be myself: A case study in rational-emotive therapy.* Buckingham, England and Philadelphia, USA: Open University Press.

*Dryden, W., & Yankura, J. (1994). *Albert Ellis.* London: Sage.

Dubois, P. (1907). *The psychic treatment of nervous disorders.* New York: Funk & Wagnalls.

*Dunlap, K. (1932). *Habits: Their making and unmaking.* New York: Liveright.

**Dyer, W. (1977). *Your erroneous zones.* New York: Avon.

*D'Zurilla, J. (1986). *Problem-solving therapy.* New York: Springer.

*Elkin, I. (1994). The NIMH treatment of depression collaborative research program: Where we began and where we are. In A. E. Bergin and S. L. Garfield, eds. *Handbook of psychotherapy and behavior change.* (pp.114-139). New York: Wiley.

*Elkin, I., Shea, M. T., Watkins, J. T., Imber, S. D., Glass, D. R., Pilkonis, P. A., Leber, W. R., Doherty, W. R., Fiester, S. J., & Parloff, M. B. (1989). National Institute of Mental Health Treatment of Depression Collaborative Research Program: General effectiveness of treatments. *Archives of General Psychiatry. 46,*971-982.

*Elliott, J. E. (1993). Using releasing statements to challenge shoulds. *Journal of Cognitive Psychotherapy, 7,* 291-295.

****Ellis, A. (1957a). *How to live with a neurotic: At home and at work.* New York: Crown, rev. ed., Hollywood, CA: Wilshire Books, 1975.**

***Ellis, A. (1957b). Outcome of employing three techniques of psychotherapy. *Journal of Clinical Psychology, 13,* 344-350.**

***Ellis, A. (1958). Rational psychotherapy. *Journal of General Psychology, 59,* 35-49. Reprinted: New York: Institute for Rational-Emotive Therapy.**

*Ellis, A. (1959). Requisite conditions for basic personality change. *Journal of Consulting Psychology, 23,* 538-540.

****Ellis, A (1960). *The Art and Science of Love.* New York: Lyle Stuart and Bantam.**

***Ellis, A. (1962). *Reason and emotion in psychotherapy.* Secaucus, NJ: Citadel. Rev. ed., Secaucus, NJ: Carol Publishing Group, 1994.**

*Ellis, A. (1965a). *The treatment of borderline and psychotic individuals.* New York: Institute for Rational-Emotive Therapy. Rev. ed., 1989.

*Ellis, A. (1965b). Workshop in rational-emotive therapy. Institute for Rational-Emotive Therapy, New York City, September 8.

*Ellis, A. (1967). Goals of psychotherapy. In A. H. Mahrer, ed. *The goals of psychotherapy* (pp.206-220). New York: Macmillan.

*Ellis, A. (1968). Is psychoanalysis harmful? *Psychiatric Opinion, 5,* 16-25. Reprinted: New York: Institute for Rational-Emotive Therapy.

*Ellis, A. (1969). A weekend of rational encounter. *Rational Living, 4*(2), 1-8. Reprinted in A. Ellis & W. Dryden, *The practice of rational-emotive therapy* (pp. 180-191). New York: Springer, 1987.

*Ellis, A. (1971). *Growth through reason*. North Hollywood, CA: Wilshire Books.

*Ellis, A. (1972a). Helping people get better rather than merely feel better. *Rational Living, 7*(2), 2-9.

**Ellis, A. (1972b). *Executive leadership: The rational-emotive approach*. New York: Institute for Rational-Emotive Therapy.

*Ellis, A. (1972c). Emotional education in the classroom: The living school. *Journal of Clinical and Child Psychology, 1*(3), 19-22.

*Ellis, A. (1972d). *Psychotherapy and the value of a human being*. New York: Institute for Rational-Emotive Therapy. Reprinted in A. Ellis & W. Dryden, *The Essential Albert Ellis*. New York: Springer, 1990.

**Ellis, A. (1972e). *How to master your fear of flying*. New York: Institute for Rational-Emotive Therapy.

**Ellis, A., speaker. (1973a). *How to stubbornly refuse to be ashamed of anything*. Cassette recording. New York: Institute for Rational-Emotive Therapy.

*Ellis, A. (1973b). *Humanistic psychotherapy: The rational-emotive approach*. New York: McGraw-Hill.

**Ellis, A., speaker. (1973c). *Twenty-one ways to stop worrying*. Cassette recording. New York: Institute for Rational-Emotive Therapy.

*Ellis, A. (1974a). Cognitive aspects of abreactive therapy. *Voices, 10*(1), 48-56. Reprinted: New York: Institute for Rational-Emotive Therapy. Rev. ed., 1992.

**Ellis, A., speaker. (1974b). *Rational living in an irrational world*. Cassette recording. New York: Institute for Rational-Emotive Therapy.

*Ellis, A. (1974c). *Techniques of disputing irrational beliefs (DIBS)*. New York: Institute for Rational-Emotive Therapy.

**Ellis, A. (1975a). *How to live with a neurotic*. Rev. ed. North Hollywood, CA: Wilshire Books.

**Ellis, A., speaker. (1975b). *RET and assertiveness training*. Cassette recording. New York: Institute for Rational-Emotive Therapy.

Ellis, A (1976a). *Sex and the Liberated Man*. Secaucus, NJ: Lyle Stuart.

*Ellis, A. (1976b). The biological basis of human irrationality. *Journal of Individual Psychology, 32*, 145-168. Reprinted: New York: Institute for Rational-Emotive Therapy.

**Ellis, A., speaker, (1976c). *Conquering low frustration tolerance*. Cassette recording. New York: Institute for Rational-Emotive Therapy.

*Ellis, A. (1976d). RET abolishes most of the human ego. *Psychotherapy, 13*, 343-348. Reprinted: New York: Institute for Rational-Emotive Therapy. Rev. ed., 1991.

**Ellis, A. (1977a). *Anger — how to live with and without it.* Secaucus, NJ: Citadel Press.

**Ellis, A., speaker. (1977b). *Conquering the dire need for love.* Cassette recording. New York: Institute for Rational-Emotive Therapy.

*Ellis, A. (1977c). Fun as psychotherapy. *Rational Living, 12*(1), 2-6. Also: Cassette recording. New York: Institute for Rational-Emotive Therapy.

**Ellis, A., speaker. (1977d). *A garland of rational humorous songs.* Cassette recording and songbook. New York: Institute for Rational-Emotive Therapy.

**Ellis, A. (1978). *I'd like to stop but...Dealing with addictions.* Cassette recording. New York: Institute for Rational-Emotive Therapy.

**Ellis, A. (1979a). *The intelligent woman's guide to dating and mating.* Secaucus, NJ: Lyle Stuart.

*Ellis, A. (1979b). Discomfort anxiety: A new cognitive behavioral construct. Part 1. *Rational Living, 14*(2), 3-8.

*Ellis, A. (1979c). A note on the treatment of agoraphobia with cognitive modification versus prolonged exposure. *Behavior Research and Therapy, 17*, 162-164.

*Ellis, A. (1979d). Rational-emotive therapy: Research data that support the clinical and personality hypotheses of RET and other modes of cognitive-behavior therapy. In A. Ellis & J. M. Whiteley, eds. *Theoretical and empirical foundations of rational-emotive therapy* (pp. 101-173). Monterey, CA: Brooks/Cole.

*Ellis, A. (1979e). Rejoinder: Elegant and inelegant RET. In A. Ellis & J. M. Whiteley, *Theoretical and empirical foundations of rational-emotive therapy* (pp. 240-267). Monterey, CA: Brooks/Cole Publishing.

*Ellis, A. (1980a). Discomfort anxiety: A new cognitive behavioral construct. Part 2. *Rational Living, 15*(1), 25-30.

*Ellis, A. (1980b). Rational-emotive therapy and cognitive behavior therapy: Similarities and differences. *Cognitive Therapy and Research, 4*, 325-340.

**Ellis, A., speaker. (1980c). *Twenty-two ways to brighten up your love life.* Cassette recording. New York: Institute for Rational-Emotive Therapy.

*Ellis, A. (1980d). The value of efficiency in psychotherapy. *Psychotherapy, 17*, 414-419. Reprinted in A. Ellis & W. Dryden, (1990). The essential Albert Ellis (pp. 237-247). New York: Springer.

*Ellis, A. (1980e). Psychotherapy and atheistic values. *Journal of Consulting and Clinical Psychology, 48*, 635-639.

*Ellis, A. (1981). The use of rational humorous songs in psychotherapy. *Voices, 16*(4), 29-36.

**Ellis, A., speaker. (1982). *Solving emotional problems.* Cassette recording. New York: Institute for Rational-Emotive Therapy.

*Ellis, A. (1983a). *The case against religiosity.* New York: Institute for Rational-Emotive Therapy. Rev. ed., 1991.

*Ellis, A. (1983b). Failures in rational-emotive therapy. In E. B. Foa and P. M. G. Emmelkamp, eds. *Failures in behavior therapy* (pp. 159-171). New York: Wiley.

*Ellis, A. (1983c). The philosophic implications and dangers of some popular behavior therapy techniques. In M. Rosenbaum, C. M. Franks & Y. Jaffe, eds. *Perspectives in behavior therapy in the eighties* (pp. 138-151). New York: Springer.

*Ellis, A. (1984a). Introduction to H. S. Young, *The work of Howard S. Young.* Edited by W. Dryden. *British Journal of Cognitive Psychotherapy, Special Issue, 2*(2), 1-5.

*Ellis, A. (1984b). The place of meditation in cognitive-behavior therapy and rational-emotive therapy. In D. H. Shapiro & R. Walsh, eds. *Meditation* (pp. 671-673). New York: Aldine.

*Ellis, A. (1984c). The use of hypnosis with rational-emotive therapy. *International Journal of Eclectic Psychotherapy, 3*(3), 15-22.

Ellis, A. (1985a). *Overcoming resistance: Rational-emotive therapy with difficult clients.* New York: Springer.

*Ellis, A. (1985b). *Intellectual fascism.* New York: Institute for Rational-Emotive Therapy. Rev., 1991.

*Ellis, A. (1985c). A rational-emotive approach to acceptance and its relationship to EAPs. In S. H. Klarreich, J. L. Francek, & C. E. Moore, eds. *The human resources management handbook* (pp. 325-333). New York: Praeger.

*Ellis, A. (1986a). Anxiety about anxiety: The use of hypnosis with rational-emotive therapy. In E. T. Dowd & J. M. Healy, eds. *Case studies in hypnotherapy* (pp. 3-11). New York: Guilford.

**Ellis, A., speaker. (1986b). *Effective self-assertion.* Cassette recording. Washington, DC: Psychology Today Tapes.

*Ellis, A. (1986c). Rational-emotive therapy applied to relationship therapy. *Journal of Rational-Emotive Therapy,* 4-21.

*Ellis, A. (1987a). The evolution of rational-emotive therapy (RET) and cognitive-behavior therapy (CBT). In J. K. Zeig, *The evolution of psychotherapy* (pp. 107-132). New York: Brunner/Mazel.

*Ellis, A. (1987b). The impossibility of achieving consistently good mental health. *American Psychologist, 42,* 364-375.

*Ellis, A. (1987c). Integrative developments in rational-emotive therapy (RET). *Journal of Integrative and Eclectic Psychotherapy, 6,* 470-479.

*Ellis, A. (1987d). A sadly neglected cognitive element in depression. *Cognitive Therapy and Research, 11,* 121-146.

*Ellis, A. (1987e). The use of rational humorous songs in psychotherapy. In W. F. Fry, Jr. & W. A. Salamed, eds. *Handbook of humor and psychotherapy* (pp. 265-287). Sarasota, FL: Professional Resource Exchange.

*Ellis, A. (1988a). *How to stubbornly refuse to make yourself miserable about anything yes, anything!* Secaucus, NJ: Lyle Stuart.

**Ellis, A. (1988b). How to live with a neurotic man. *Journal of Rational-Emotive and Cognitive-Behavior Therapy, 6*, 129-136.

**Ellis, A., speaker. (1988c). *Unconditionally accepting yourself and others.* Cassette recording. New York: Institute for Rational-Emotive Therapy.

*Ellis, A. (1989a). Comments on my critics. In M. E. Bernard & R. DiGiuseppe, eds. *Inside rational-emotive therapy* (pp.199-233). San Diego, CA: Academic Press.

*Ellis, A. (1989b). Comments on Sandra Warnock's "Rational-Emotive Therapy and the Christian client." *Journal of Rational-Emotive & Cognitive-Behavior Therapy, 7*, 275-277.

*Ellis, A. (1989c). The history of cognition in psychotherapy. In A. Freeman, K. M. Simon, L. E. Beutler & H. Aronowitz, eds. *Comprehensive handbook of cognitive therapy* (pp. 5-19). New York: Plenum.

**Ellis, A., speaker. (1989d). *Overcoming the influence of the past.* Cassette recording. New York: Institute for Rational-Emotive Therapy.

*Ellis, A. (1989e). *The treatment of psychotic and borderline individuals with RET.* (Orig. publication, 1965). New York: Institute for Rational-Emotive Therapy.

*Ellis, A. (1989f). Using rational-emotive therapy (RET) as crisis intervention: A single session with a suicidal client. *Individual Psychology, 45*(1 & 2), 75-81.

**Ellis, A., speaker. (1990a). *Albert Ellis live at the Learning Annex.* 2 cassettes. New York: Institute for Rational-Emotive Therapy.

*Ellis, A. (1990b). Is rational-emotive therapy (RET) "rationalist" or "constructivist"? In Ellis, A., & Dryden, W., *The essential Albert Ellis* (pp. 114-141). New York: Springer.

*Ellis, A. (1990c). Let's not ignore individuality. *American Psychologist, 45* 781.

*Ellis, A. (1990d). My life in clinical psychology. In C. E. Walker, eds. *History of clinical psychology in autobiography.* Homewood, IL: Dorsey.

*Ellis, A. (1990e). Rational and irrational beliefs in counseling psychology. *Journal of Rational-Emotive and Cognitive-Behavior Therapy.*

*Ellis, A. (1990f). Special features of rational-emotive therapy. In W. Dryden & R. DiGiuseppe, *A primer of rational-emotive therapy* (pp. 79-93). Champaign, IL: Research Press.

*Ellis, A. (1991a). Achieving self-actualization. *Journal of Social Behavior and Personality, 6*(5), 1-18. Reprinted: New York: Institute for Rational-Emotive Therapy.

*Ellis, A. (1991b). Are all methods of counseling and psychotherapy equally effective? *New York State Association for Counseling and Development Journal, 6*(2), 9-13.

*Ellis, A. (1991c). *Cognitive aspects of abreactive therapy*, rev. ed. New York: Institute for Rational-Emotive Therapy.

*Ellis, A. (1991d). How can psychological treatment aim to be briefer and better. The rational-emotive approach to brief therapy. In K. N. Anchor, ed. *The handbook of medical psychotherapy* (pp. 51-88). Toronto: Hografe & Huber. Also in J. K. Zeig & S. G. Gilligan, eds. *Brief therapy: Myths, methods and metaphors* (pp. 291-302). New York: Brunner/Mazel.

**Ellis, A., speaker. (1991e). How to get along with difficult people. Cassette recording. New York: Institute for Rational-Emotive Therapy.

**Ellis, A., speaker. (1991f). *How to refuse to be angry, vindictive, and unforgiving*. Cassette recording. New York: Institute for Rational-Emotive Therapy.

*Ellis, A. (1991g). *Humanism and psychotherapy: A revolutionary approach*, rev. ed. New York: Institute for Rational-Emotive Therapy. Original publication, 1972.

*Ellis, A. (1991h). The philosophical basis of rational-emotive therapy (RET). *Psychotherapy In Private Practice, 8*(4), 97-106.

*Ellis, A. (1991i). *Rational-emotive family therapy*. In A. M. Horne & J. L. Passmore, eds. *Family counseling and therapy*, 2nd edition (pp. 403-434). Itasca, IL: F. E. Peacock.

*Ellis, A. (1991j). The revised ABCs of rational-emotive therapy. In J. Zeig, ed. *The evolution of psychotherapy: The second conference* (pp. 79-99). New York: Brunner/Mazel. Expanded version: *Journal of Rational-Emotive and Cognitive-Behavior Therapy, 9*, 139-172.

**Ellis, A. (1991k). *Self-management workbook: Strategies for personal success*. New York: Institute for Rational-Emotive Therapy.

*Ellis, A. (1991l). Suggestibility, irrational beliefs, and emotional disturbance. In J. F. Schumaner, ed. *Human suggestibility* (pp. 309-325). New York: Routledge.

*Ellis, A. (1991m). Using RET effectively: Reflections and interview. In M. E. Bernard, ed. *Using rational-emotive therapy effectively* (pp. 1-33). New York: Plenum.

*Ellis, A. (1992a). Brief therapy: The rational-emotive method. In S. H. Budman, M. F. Hoyt, & S. Fiedman, eds. *The first session in brief therapy* (pp. 36-58). New York: Guilford.

*Ellis, A. (1992b). Foreword to Paul Hauck, *Overcoming the rating game* (pp. 1-4). Louisville, KY: Westminster/John Knox.

Ellis, A., speaker. (1992c). *How to age with style.* Cassette recording. New York: Institute for Rational-Emotive Therapy.

*Ellis, A. (1992d). Group rational-emotive and cognitive-behavioral therapy. *International Journal of Group Psychotherapy, 42,* 63-80.

*Ellis, A. (1992e). My current views on rational-emotive therapy (RET) and religiousness. *Journal of Rational-Emotive and Cognitive-Behavior Therapy, 10,* 37-40.

*Ellis, A. (1992f). Rational-emotive approaches to peace. *Journal of Cognitive Psychotherapy, 6,* 79-104.

*Ellis, A. (1993a). Changing rational-emotive therapy (RET) to rational emotive behavior therapy (REBT). *Behavior Therapist, 16,* **257-258.**

*Ellis, A. (1993b). Rational emotive imagery: RET version. In M. E. Bernard & J. L. Wolfe, eds. *The RET source book for practitioners* **(pp. II8-II10). New York: Institute for Rational-Emotive Therapy.**

*Ellis, A., speaker. (1993c). *Coping with the suicide of a loved one.* Video cassette. New York: Institute for Rational-Emotive Therapy.

*Ellis, A. (1993d). Fundamentals of rational-emotive therapy for the 1990s. In W. Dryden & L.K. Hill, eds. *Innovations in rational-emotive therapy* (pp. 1-32). Newbury Park, CA: Sage Publications.

*Ellis, A. (1993e). General semantics and rational emotive behavior therapy. *Bulletin of General Semantics,* No. 58, 12-28. Also in P. D. Johnston, D. D. Bourland, Jr., & J. Klein, eds. *More E-prime* (pp. 213-240). Concord, CA: International Society for General Semantics.

**Ellis, A., speaker. (1993f). *How to be a perfect non-perfectionist.* Cassette recording. New York: Institute for Rational-Emotive Therapy.

**Ellis, A., speaker. (1993g). *Living fully and in balance: This isn't a dress rehearsal. This is it!* Cassette recording. New York: Institute for Rational-Emotive Therapy.

*Ellis, A. (1993h). Rational-emotive therapy and hypnosis. In J. W. Rhue, S. J. Lynn, & I. Kirsh, eds. *Handbook of clinical hypnosis* (pp. 173-186). Washington, DC: American Psychological Association.

*Ellis, A. (1993i). The rational-emotive therapy (RET) approach to marriage and family therapy. *Family Journal: Counseling and Therapy for Couples and Families, 1,* 292-307.

*Ellis, A. (1993j). The advantages and disadvantages of self-help therapy materials. *Professional Psychology: Research and Practice, 24,* 335-339.

*Ellis, A. (1993k). Reflections on rational-emotive therapy. *Journal of Consulting and Clinical Psychology, 61,* 199-201.

**Ellis, A., speaker. (1993l). *Releasing your creative energy.* Cassette recording. New York: Institute for Rational-Emotive Therapy.

*Ellis, A. (1993m). Vigorous RET disputing. In M. E. Bernard & J. L. Wolfe, eds. *The RET resource book for practitioners* (pp. II7). New York: Institute for Rational-Emotive Therapy.

*Ellis, A., speaker. (1993n). *Rational-emotive approach to brief therapy*. 2 cassette recordings. Phoenix, AZ: Milton Erickson Foundation.

*Ellis, A. (1994a). *Reason and emotion in psychotherapy*. Revised and updated. New York: Birch Lane Press.

*Ellis, A. (1994b). Post-traumatic stress disorder (PTSD) in rape victims: A rational emotive behavioral theory. *Journal of Rational-Emotive and Cognitive-Behavior Therapy, 12*, 3-25.

*Ellis, A. (1994c). Radical behavioral treatment of private events: A response to Michael Dougher. *Behavior Therapist, 17*, 219-221.

*Ellis, A. (1994d). Rational emotive behavior therapy approaches to obsessive-compulsive disorder (OCD). *Journal of Rational-Emotive Therapy. Emotive and Cognitive-Behavior Therapy, 12*, 121-141.

*Ellis, A. (1994e). Foreword to P. D. Johnston, D. D. Bourland, Jr., & J. Klein, eds. *More E-prime* (pp. xiii-xviii). Concord, CA: International Society for General Semantics.

*Ellis, A. (1994f). Secular humanism. In F. Wertz, ed. *The humanistic movement* (pp. 233-242). Lakeworth, FL: Gardner Press.

*Ellis, A. (1994g). The treatment of borderline personalities with rational emotive behavior therapy. *Journal of Rational-Emotive and Cognitive-Behavior Therapy, 12* 101-119.

*Ellis, A. (1994h). Life in a box. Review of D. W. Bjork, *B. F. Skinner: A Life. Readings, 9*(4), 16-21.

*Ellis, A. (1994i). The sport of avoiding sports and exercise. *Sport Psychologist, 8*, 240-261.

*Ellis, A. (1995a). A social constructionist position for mental health couseling: A response to Jeffrey A. Guterman. *Journal of Mental Health Counseling*.

*Ellis, A. (1995b, March 6). Dogmatic religion doesn't help, it hurts. *Insight in The News*, pp. 20-22.

*Ellis, A. (1996). *Better, deeper, and more enduring therapy*. New York: Brunner/Mazel.

*Ellis, A. (1997). Postmodern ethics for active-directive counseling and psychotherapy. *Journal of Mental Health Counseling, 18*, 211-225.

*Ellis, A., & Abrahms, E. (1978). *Brief psychotherapy in medical and health practice*. New York: Springer.

**Ellis, A., & Abrams, M. (1994). *How to cope with a fatal disease*. New York: Barricade Books.

**Ellis, A., Abrams, M., & Dengelegi, L. (1992). *The art and science of rational eating*. New York: Barricade Books.

**Ellis, A., & Becker, I. (1982). *A guide to personal happiness.* North Hollywood, CA: Wilshire Books.

*Ellis, A., & Bernard, M.E., eds. (1983). *Rational-emotive approaches to the problems of childhood.* New York: Plenum.

*Ellis, A., & Bernard, M. E., eds. (1985b). *Clinical applications of rational-emotive therapy.* New York: Plenum.

*Ellis, A., & DiGiuseppe, R., speaker. (1994). *Dealing with addictions.* Videotape. New York: Institute for Rational-Emotive Therapy.

**Ellis, A., & DiMattia, D. (1991). *Self-management: Strategies for personal success.* New York: Institute for rational-Emotive Therapy.

*Ellis, A., & Dryden, W. (1985). Dilemmas in giving warmth or love to clients: An interview with Windy Dryden. In W. Dryden, *Therapists' Dilemmas* (pp. 5-16). London: Harper & Row.

*Ellis, A., & Dryden, W. (1987). The practice of rational-emotive therapy. New York: Springer.

*Ellis, A., & Dryden, W. (1990). The essential Albert Ellis. New York: Springer.

*Ellis, A., & Dryden, W. (1991). *A dialogue with Albert Ellis: Against dogma.* Philadelphia: Open University Press.

*Ellis, A., & Dryden, W. (1993). A therapy by any other name? An interview. *The Rational Emotive Therapist,* 1(2), 34-37.

*Ellis, A. & Dryden, W. (1997). *The practice of rational emotive behavior therapy.* Rev. ed., New York: Springer.

*Ellis, A. Gordon, J., Neenan, M. & Palmer, S. (1997). *Stress Counseling: A rational emotive behavior approach.* London: Cassell and New York: Springer.

*Ellis, A., & Grieger, R., eds. (1977). *Handbook of rational-emotive therapy,* vol. 1. New York: Springer.

*Ellis, A., & Grieger, R., eds. (1986). *Handbook of rational-emotive therapy,* vol. 2. New York: Springer.

**Ellis, A., & Harper, R. A. (1961). *A guide to successful marriage.* North Hollywood, CA: Wilshire Books.

**Ellis, A., & Harper, R. A. (1997). *A guide to rational living.* 3rd Rev. ed., North Hollywood, CA: Melvin Powers.

**Ellis, A., & Hunter, P. (1991). *Why am I always broke?* New York: Carol Publications.

**Ellis, A., & Knaus, W. (1977). *Overcoming procrastination.* New York: New American Library.

*Ellis, A., Krasner, P., & Wilson, R. A. (1960). An impolite interview with Dr. Albert Ellis. *Realist,* Issue *16,* 1, 9-14; Issue *17,* 7-12. Rev. ed., New York: Institute for Rational-Emotive Therapy. Rev. ed., 1985.

**Ellis, A., & Lange, A. (1994). *How to keep people from pushing your buttons.* New York: Carol Publishing.

*Ellis, A., McInerny, J. F., DiGiuseppe, R., & Yeager, R. J. (1988). *Rational-emotive therapy with alcoholics and substance abusers.* Needham, MA: Allyn & Bacon.

*Ellis, A., & Robb, H. (1994). Acceptance in rational-emotive therapy. In S. C. Hayes, N. S. Jacobson, V. M. Follette, & M. J. Dougher, eds. *Acceptance and change: Content and context in psychotherapy* (pp. 91-102). Reno, NV: Context Press.

*Ellis, A., Sichel, J., Leaf, R. C., & Mass, R. (1989). Countering perfectionism in research on clinical practice. I: Surveying rationality changes after a single intensive RET intervention. *Journal of Rational-Emotive & Cognitive-Behavior Therapy, 7,* 197-218.

Ellis, A., Sichel, J. L., Yeager, R. J., DiMattia, D. J., & DiGiuseppe, R. A. (1989). *Rational-emotive couples therapy.* Needham, MA: Allyn & Bacon.

Ellis, A., & Velten, E. (1992). *When AA doesn't work for you: Rational steps for quitting alcohol.* New York: Barricade Books.

*Ellis, A., & Whiteley, J. M. (1979). *Theoretical and empirical foundations of rational-emotive therapy.* Monterey, CA: Brooks/Cole.

**Ellis, A., Wolfe, J. L., & Moseley, S. (1966). *How to raise an emotionally healthy, happy child.* North Hollywood, CA: Wilshire Books.

*Ellis, A., & Yeager, R. (1989). *Why some therapies don't work: The dangers of transpersonal psychology.* Buffalo, NY: Prometheus.

*Ellis, A., Young, J., & Lockwood, G. (1987). Cognitive therapy and rational emotive therapy: A dialogue. *Journal of Cognitive Psychotherapy, 1*(4), 137-187.

*Engels, G. I., Garnefski, N., Diekstra, R. F. W. (1993). Efficacy of rational-emotive therapy: A quantitative analysis. *Journal of Consulting and Clinical Psychology, 61,* 1083-1090.

Epictetus. (1899). *The collected works of Epictetus.* Boston: Little, Brown.

*Epicurus (1994). *Letter on happiness.* San Francisco: Chronicle Books.

**Epstein, S. (1993). *You're smarter than you think.* New York: Simon & Schuster.

*Epstein, S. (1994). Integration of the cognitive and the psychodynamic unconscious. *American Psychologist, 49,* 709.

*Eysenck, M. W. (1992). *Anxiety: The cognitive perspective.* Hillside, NJ: Erlbaum.

Fava, M., Bless, E., Otto, M. W., Pava, A., et al. (1994). Dysfunctional attitudes in major depression: Change with pharmacotherapy. *Journal of Nervous & Mental Disease, 182,* 45-49.

Feyerband, P. (1975). *Against method.* New York: Humanistics Press.

*FitzMaurice, K. (1989). *Self-concept: The enemy within.* Omaha, NE: FitzMaurice Publishing Co.

*FitzMaurice, K. (1991). *We're all insane.* Omaha, NE: Palmtree Publishers.

*FitzMaurice, K. (1994). *Introducing the 12 steps of emotional disturbances.* Omaha, NE: Autor.

**Foa, E. B. & Wilson, R. (1991). *Stop obsessing: How to overcome your obsessions and compulsions.* New York: Bantam.

*Forest, J. (1987). Effects of self-actualization of paperbacks about psychological self-help. *Psychological Reports, 60,* 1243-1246.

Frank, J. (1985). Therapeutic components shared by all psychotherapies. In M. Mahoney & A. Freeman, eds. *Cognition and psychotherapy* (pp. 49-79). New York: Plenum.

*Frank, J. D., & Frank, J. B. (1991). *Persuasion and healing.* Baltimore, MD: Johns Hopkins University Press.

*Frankl, V. (1959). *Man's search for meaning.* New York: Pocket Books.

*Franklin, R. (1993). *Overcoming the myth of self-worth.* Appleton, WI: Focus Press.

*Freeman, A. (1994). *Short-term therapy for the long-term patient: Workshop syllabus.* Chapel Hill, NJ: Author.

*Freeman, A., & Dattillo, F. W. (1992). *Comprehensive casebook of cognitive therapy.* New York: Plenum.

**Freeman, A., & DeWolfe, R. (1993). *The ten dumbest mistakes smart people make and how to avoid them.* New York: Harper Perennial.

Freud, S. (1965). *Standard edition of the complete psychological works of Sigmund Freud.* New York: Basic Books.

*Fried, R. (1993). *The psychology and physiology of breathing.* New York: Plenum.

*Friedman, M. I., & Lackey, G. H., Jr. (1991). *The psychology of human control.* New York: Praeger.

**Froggatt, W. (1993). *Choose to be happy.* New Zealand: Harper-Collins.

*Gelber, D. M. (1993). Re: Exposure therapy. *Behavior Therapist, 16*(2), 13.

*Gerald, M., & Eyman, W. (1981). *Thinking straight and talking sense: An emotional education program.* New York: Institute for Rational-Emotive Therapy.

Gergen, R. J. (1991). *The saturated self.* New York: Basic Books.

Glass, C.R., & Arnkoff, D.B. (1997). Questionnaire methods of cognitive self-statement assessment. *Journal of Consulting and Clinical Psychology, 65,* 971-927.

Glasser, W. (1965). *Reality therapy.* New York: Harper & Row.

*Glasser, W. (1992a). Reality therapy. In J. K. Zeig, ed. *The evolution of psychotherapy: The second conference* (pp. 270-282). New York: Brunner/Mazel.

*Glasser, W. (1992b). Discussion of Jay Haley, *Zen and the art of therapy.* In J.K. Zeig, ed., *The evolution of psychotherapy: The second conference* (pp. 34-35). New York: Brunner/Mazel.

*Golden, W. L., Dowd, E. T., & Friedberg, F. (1987). *Hypnotherapy: A modern approach*. New York: Pergamon.

*Goldfried, M. R., & Castonguay, L. G. (1993). Behavior therapy: Redefining strengths and limitations. *Behavior Therapy, 24*, 505-526.

*Goldfried, M. R., & Davison, G. C. (1991). *Clinical behavior therapy*, 3rd ed. New York: Holt Rinehart & Winston.

Goldsmith, T. H. (1991). *The biological roots of human nature*. New York: Oxford.

*Goleman, D. (1989, July 6). Feeling gloomy? A good self-help book may actually help. *New York Times*, p. B6.

*Goleman, D. (1993, March 21). A slow methodical calming of the mind. *New York Times Magazine*, p. 20-21.

**Gordon, S. (1994). *"Is there anything I can do?" Helping a friend when times are tough*. New York: Delacorte.

*Gould, R. A., Clum, G. A., & Shapiro, D. (1993). The use of bibliotherapy in the treatment of panic: A preliminary investigation. *Behavior Therapy, 24*, 241-252.

*Goulding, M. M. (1992). Short-term redecision therapy in the treatment of clients who suffered childhood abuse. In J. Zeig, ed. *The evolution of psychotherapy: The second conference* (pp. 239-251). New York: Brunner/Mazel.

*Granvold, D. K., ed. (1994). *Cognitive and behavioral treatment: Methods and applications*. Pacific Grove, CA: Brooks/Cole.

*Greenberg, L. S., & Safran, J. D. (1987). *Emotion in psychotherapy*. New York: Guilford.

*Greenwald, H. (1987). *Direct decision therapy*. San Diego, CA: Edits.

*Greist, J. H. (1993). *Obsessive compulsive disorder*. Madison, WI: Dean Foundation for Health and Education.

*Grieger, R. M. (1988). From a linear to a contextual model of the ABCs of RET. In W. Dryden and P. Trower, eds. *Developments in cognitive psychotherapy* (pp. 71-105). London: Sage.

*Grieger, R., & Boyd, J. (1980). *Rational-emotive therapy: A skills-based approach*. New York: Van Nostrand Reinhold.

**Grieger, R. M., & Woods, P. J. (1993). *The rational-emotive therapy companion*. Roanoke, VA: Scholars Press.

*Grossack, M. (1976). *Love and reason*. Boston: Institute for Rational Living.

Guidano, V. F. (1991). *The self in progress*. New York: Guilford.
Guterman, J. T. (1994). A social constructionist position for mental health counseling. *Journal of Mental Health Counseling, 16*, 226-244.

*Haaga, D. A., & Davison, G. C. (1989). Outcome studies of rational-emotive therapy. In M. E. Bernard & R. DiGiuseppe, eds. *Inside rational-emotive therapy* (pp. 155-197). San Diego, CA: Academic Press.

*Hajzler, D., & Bernard, M. E. (1991). A review of rational-emotive outcome studies. *School Psychology Quarterly, 6*(1), 27-49.

*Haley, J. (1963). *Strategies of psychotherapy.* New York: Grune & Stratton.

*Haley, J. (1990). *Problem solving therapy.* San Francisco: Jossey-Bass.

*Hammond, D. C., & Stanfield, K. (1977). *Multi-dimensional psychotherapy.* Chicago: Institute for Personality and Ability Testing.

**Hauck, P. A. (1973). *Overcoming depression.* Philadelphia: Westminster.

**Hauck, P. A. (1974). *Overcoming frustration and anger.* Philadelphia: Westminster.

**Hauck, P. A. (1977). *Marriage is a loving business.* Philadelphia: Westminster.

**Hauck, P. A. (1991). *Overcoming the rating game: Beyond self-love, beyond self-esteem.* Louisville, KY: Westminster/John Knox.

Hayes, S.C. (1987). A contextual approach to therapeutic change. In N. Jacobson , ed. *Therapists in clinical practice* (p.327-386) New York: Guilford.

*Hayes, S. C. (1995). Why cognitions are not causes. *Behavior Therapist, 18,* 59-60.

*Hayes, S. C., & Hayes, L. J. (1992). Some clinical implications of contextualistic behaviorism: The example of cognition. *Behavior Therapy, 23,* 225-249.

*Hayes, S. C., McCurry, S. M., Afan, N., & Wilson, K. (1991). *Acceptance and commitment therapy (ACT).* Reno, NV: University of Nevada.

*Hayes, S. C., & Melancon, S. M. (1989). Comprehensive distancing, paradox, and the treatment of emotional avoidance. In M. Ascher, ed. *Paradoxical procedures in psychotherapy* (pp. 110-130). New York: Guilford.

Heidegger, M. (1962). *Being and time.* New York: Harper & Row.

*Herzberg, A. (1945). *Active psychotherapy.* New York: Grune & Stratton.

*Hollon, S. D., & Beck, A. T. (1994). Cognitive and cognitive/behavioral therapies. In A. E. Bergin & S. L. Garfield, eds. *Handbook of psychotherapy and behavior change* (pp.428-466). New York: Wiley.

Ivey, A.E. & Rigazio-DiGilio, S.A. (1991). Toward a developmental practice of mental health counseling: strategies for training, practice, and political unity. *Journal of Mental Health Counseling, 13,* 21-26.

*Janet, P. (1898). *Neurosis et idée fixes.* 2 vols. Paris: Alcan.

*Janis, I. L. (1983). *Short-term counseling.* New Haven, CT: Yale University Press.

*Janis, I. L., & Mann, L. (1977). *Decision making.* New York: Free Press.

**Jacobson, N. S. (1992). Behavioral couple therapy: A new beginning. *Behavior Therapy, 23,* 491-506.

*Johnson, W. (1946). *People in quandaries.* New York: Harper & Row.

*Johnson, W. R. (1981). *So desperate the fight.* New York: Institute for Rational-Emotive Therapy.

*Kanfer, F. H., & Goldstein, A. P., eds. (1986). *Helping people change.* 3rd ed. New York: Pergamon.

*Kanfer, F. H., & Schefft, B. K. (1988). *Guiding the process of therapeutic change.* New York: Pergamon.

*Kazdin, A. E. (1994). Psychotherapy for children and adolescents. In A. E. Bergin & S. L. Garfield, eds. *Handbook of psychotherapy and behavior change* (pp. 543-594). New York: Wiley.

Kelly, G. (1955). *The psychology of personal constructs.* 2 vols. New York: Norton.

Kendall, P.C., Hollon, S.D. (1980). *Assessment strategies for cognitive-behavioral interventions.* New York: Academic Press.

*Kiser, D. J., Piercy, E. P., & Lipchik, E. (1993). The integration of emotion in solution-focused therapy. *Journal of Marital and Family Therapy, 19,* 233-242.

Klein, M. (1984). *Envy and gratitude and other works.* New York: Free Press.

Klerman, G.L., Rounsville, B., Chevron, E., Neu, C. & Weissman, M. (1979). *Manual for short-term interpersonal psychotherapy (IPT) of depression.* New Haven: Boston Collaborative Depression Project.

*Knaus, W. (1974). *Rational-emotive education.* New York: Institute for Rational-Emotive Therapy.

Kohut, H. (1991). *The search for the self: selected writings of Heinz Kohut.* Madison, CT: International Universities Press.

*Kopec, A. M., Beal, D., & DiGiuseppe, R. (1994). Training in RET: Disputational strategies. *Journal of Rational-Emotive and Cognitive-Behavior Therapy, 12,*

Korzybski, A. (1933). *Science and sanity.* San Francisco: International Society of General Semantics.

*Kottler, J. A. (1991). *The complete therapist.* San Francisco: Jossey-Bass.

*Kuehlwein, K. T., & Rosen, H. eds. (1993). *Cognitive therapies in action.* San Francisco: Jossey-Bass.

*Kwee, M. G. T. (1982). Psychotherapy and the practice of general semantics. *Methodology and Science, 15,* 236-256.

*Kwee, M. (1991). Cognitive and behavioral approaches to meditation. In M. G. Kwee, *Psychotherapy, meditation and health* (pp. 36-53). London: East/West Publications.

*Kwee, M. G. T. (1991). *Psychotherapy, meditation, and health: A cognitive behavioral perspective.* London: East/West Publication.

*Lange, A., & Jakubowski, P. (1976). *Responsible assertive behavior.* Champaign, IL: Research Press.

*Laydon, M. A., & Newman, C. F. (1993). *Cognitive therapy of borderline disorder.* Des Moines, IA: Longwood Division, Allyn & Bacon.

*Lazarus, A. A. (1977). Toward an egoless state of being. In A. Ellis & R. Grieger, eds. *Handbook of rational-emotive therapy.* Vol. 1 (pp. 113-116). New York: Springer.

**Lazarus, A. A. (1985). *Marital myths.* San Luis Obispo, CA: Impact Publishers, Inc.

*Lazarus, A. A. (1989). *The practice of multimodal therapy.* Baltimore, MD: Johns Hopkins.

*Lazarus, A. A. (1992). Clinical/therapeutic effectiveness: Banning the procrustean bed and challenging 10 prevalent myths. In J. K. Zeig, ed. *The evolution of psychotherapy: The second conference* (pp. 100-113) Moines, IA: Longwood Division, Allyn & Bacon.

Lazarus, A.A., & Lazarus C.N. (1997) *The 60-second shrink.* San Luis Obispo, CA: Impact Publishers, Inc.

**Lazarus, A. A., Lazarus, C., & Fay, A. (1993). *Don't believe it for a minute: Forty toxic ideas that are driving you crazy.* San Luis Obispo, CA: Impact Publishers, Inc.

*Lazarus, R. S. (1966). *Psychological stress and the coping process.* New York: McGraw-Hill.

*Lazarus, R. S. (1994). *Emotion and adaptation.* New York: Oxford.

*Lazarus, R. S., & Folkman, S. (1984). *Stress, appraisal, and coping.* New York: Springer.

*Lazarus, R. S., & Lazarus, B. N. (1994). *Passion and reason.* New York: Oxford.

**Lewinsohn, P., Antonuccio, D., Breckenridge, J., & Teri, L. (1984). *"The coping with depression course."* Eugene, OR: Castalia.

*Levey, A. B., Aldaz, J. A., Watts, F. N., & Coyle, K. (1991). Articulatory suppression and the treatment of insomnia. *Behavior Research and Therapy, 29,* 85-89.

*Lichtenberg, J. W., Johnson, D. D., & Arachtingi, B. M. (1992). Physical illness and subscription to Ellis's irrational beliefs. *Journal of Counseling and Development, 71,* 157-163.

*Lightsey, O. R., Jr., (1994). "Thinking positive" as a stress buffer: Role of positive automatic cognitions in depression and happiness. *Journal of Counseling Psychology, 41,* 325-334.

*Linehan, M. M. (1993). *Cognitive-behavioral treatment of borderline personality disorders.* New York: Guilford.

*Lipsey, M. W., & Wilson, D. B. (1993). The efficacy of psychological, educational, and behavior treatment: Confirmation from meta-analysis. *American Psychologist, 48,* 1181-1209.

**Low, A. A. (1952). *Mental health through will training.* Boston: Christopher.

*Lyons, L. C., & Woods, P. J. (1991). The efficacy of rational-emotive therapy: A quantitative review of the outcome research. *Clinical Psychology Review, 11*, 357-369.

*Mahoney, M. J. (1991). *Human change processes.* New York: Basic Books.

*Mahoney, M. J., ed. (1995). *Cognitive and constructive psychotherapies: Theory, research and practice.* New York: Springer.

**Marcus Aurelius. (1890). *Meditations.* Boston: Little, Brown.

*Marks, I. (1994). Behavior therapy as an aid to self-care. *Current Directions in Psychological Science, 3*(1), 19-22.

*Marlatt, G. A., & Gordon, J. R., eds. (1989). *Relapse prevention: Maintenance strategies in the treatment of addictive behaviors.* New York: Guilford.

*Marmor, J. (1987). The psychotherapeutic process: Common denominators on diverse approaches. In J. Zeig, ed. *The evolution of psychotherapy* (pp. 266-282). New York: Brunner/Mazel.

*Maultsby, M. C., Jr. (1971a). Rational emotive imagery. *Rational Living, 6*(1), 24-27.

*Maultsby, M. C., Jr. (1971b). Systematic written homework in psychotherapy. *Psychotherapy, 8*, 195-198.

*Maultsby, M. C., Jr. (1984). *Rational behavior therapy.* Englewood Cliffs, NJ: Prentice-Hall.

May, R. (1969). *Love and will.* New York: Norton.

*McGovern, T. E., & Silverman, M. S. (1984). A review of outcome studies of rational-emotive therapy from 1977 to 1982. *Journal of Rational-Emotive Therapy, 2*(1), 7-18.

**McKay, G. D., & Dinkmeyer, D. (1994). *How you feel is up to you.* San Luis Obispo, CA: Impact Publishers, Inc.

*McMullin, R. (1986). *Handbook of cognitive therapy techniques.* New York: Norton.

*Meichenbaum, D. (1977). *Cognitive-behavior modification.* New York: Plenum.

*Meichenbaum, D. (1992). Evolution of cognitive behavior therapy: Origins, tenets, and clinical examples. In J. K. Zeig, ed. *The evolution of psychotherapy: The second conference* (pp. 114-128).

*Meichenbaum, D., & Cameron, R. (1983). Stress inoculation training. In D. Meichenbaum & M. E. Jaremko, eds. *Stress reduction and prevention* (pp. 115-154). New York: Plenum.

**Miller, T. (1986). *The unfair advantage.* Manlius, NY: Horsesense, Inc.

**Mills, D. (1993). *Overcoming self-esteem.* New York: Institute for Rational-Emotive Therapy.

*Neimeyer, G. J. (1993). The challenge of change: Reflections on constructive psychotherapy. *Journal of Cognitive Psychotherapy, 7*, 183-194.

*Neimeyer, R. A. (1993). Constructivism and the cognitive psychotherapies: Some conceptual and strategic contrasts. *Journal of Cognitive Psychotherapy, 7*, 159-171.

*Neimeyer, R.A. & Mahoney, M.V. (1995). *Constructivism in psychotherapy.* Washington, D.C.: American Psychological Association.

*Nezu, A. M. (1985). Differences in psychological distress between effective and ineffective problem solvers. *Journal of Counseling Psychology, 54*, 135-138.

*Nezu, A. M. (1986). Efficacy of a social problem-solving therapy approach for unipolar depression. *Journal of Consulting and Clinical Psychology, 54*, 42-48.

*Norcross, J. C., & Goldfried, M. R. (1992). *Handbook of psychotherapy integration.* New York: Basic Books.

**Nottingham, E. (1992). *It's not as bad as it seems: A thinking approach to happiness.* Memphis, TN: Castle Books.

**Nye, B. (1993). *Understanding and managing your anger and aggression.* Federal Way, WA: BCA Publishing.

*O'Hanlon, B, & Beadle, S. (1994). *A field guide to possibility land: Possibility therapy methods.* Omaha, NE: Possibility Press.

*O'Hanlon, B., & Wilk, J. (1987). *Shifting contexts: The generation of effective psychotherapy.* New York: Guilford.

*Olkin, R. (1994). The use of a paradoxical intervention for the treatment of recalcitrant temper tantrums. *Behavior Therapist, 17*, 37-40.

*Palmer, S., Dryden, W., Ellis, A., & Yapp, R. (1995). *Rational interviews.* London: Centre for Rational Emotive Behavior Therapy.

*Palmer, S., & Ellis, A. (1994). In the counselor's chair. *The Rational Emotive Therapist, 2*(1), 6-15. From *Counseling Journal*, 1993, 4, 171-174.

Paul, G. L. (1967). Strategy of outcome research in psychotherapy. *Journal of Consulting Psychology, 31*, 108-118.

**Peale, N. V. (1952). *The power of positive thinking.* New York: Fawcett.

Perls, F. (1969). *Gestalt therapy verbatim.* New York: Delta.

*Peterson, C., Maier, S. F., & Seligman, M. E. P. (1993). *Learned helplessness.* New York: Oxford.

*Phadke, K. M. (1982). Some innovations in RET theory and practice. *Rational Living, 17*(2), 25-30.

*Phillips, E. L., & Wiener, D. N. (1966). *Short-term psychotherapy and structured behavior change.* New York: McGraw-Hill.

*Pietsch. W. V. (1993). *The serenity prayer.* San Francisco: Harper San Francisco.

*Plutchik, R., & Kelerman, H. (1990). *Emotion, psychopathology, and psychotherapy.* San Diego, CA: Academic Press.

Popper, K. R. (1985). *Popper selections.* ed. by David Miller. Princeton, NJ: University Press.

**Powell, J. (1976). *Fully human, fully alive.* Niles, IL: Argus.

*Prochaska, J. O., DiClemente, C. C., & Norcross, J. C. (1992). In search of how people change: Applications to addictive behaviors. *American Psychologist, 47,* 1102-1114.

*Raimy, V. (1975). *Misunderstandings of the self.* San Francisco: Jossey-Bass.

Reich, W. (1960). *Selected writings.* **New York: Farrar, Straus and Cudahy.**

*Robin, M. W., & DiGiuseppe, R. (1993). Rational-emotive therapy with an avoidant personality. In K. T. Kuehlwein & H. Rosen, eds. *Cognitive therapies in action* (pp. 143-159).

Rogers, C. R. (1957). The necessary and sufficient conditions of therapeutic personality change. *Journal of Consulting Psychology, 21,* **95-103.**

Rogers, C R. (1961). *On becoming a person.* **Boston: Houghton-Mifflin.**

*Rorer, L. G. (1989). Rational-emotive theory: I. An integrated psychological and philosophic basis. II. Explication and evaluation. *Cognitive Therapy and Research, 13,* 75-492; 531-548.

*Rotter, J. B. (1954). *Social learning and clinical psychology.* Englewood Cliffs, NJ: Prentice-Hall.

*Rush, A. J. (1989). The therapeutic alliance in short-term cognitive-behavior therapy. In W. Dryden & P. Trower, eds. *Cognitive psychotherapy: Stasis and change* (pp. 59-72). London: Cassell.

**Russell, B. (1950). *The conquest of happiness.* New York: New American Library.

*Safran, J. D., & Greenberg, L. S., eds. (1991). *Emotion, psychotherapy, and change.* New York: Guilford.

*Salter, A. (1949). *Conditioned reflex therapy.* New York: Creative Age. Sampson, E. E. (1989) The challenge of social change in psychology. Globalization and psychology's theory of the person. *American Psychologist, 44,* 914-921.

Sampson, E.E. (1989) The challenge of social change in psychology. Globalization and psychology's theory of the person. *American Psychologist,* **44, 914-921.**

*Satir, V. (1978). *People making.* Palo Alto: Science & Behavior Books.

*Schwartz, R. (1993). The idea of balance and integrative psychotherapy. *Journal of Psychotherapy Integration, 3,* 159-181.

Schwartz, R.B. (1997). Consider the simple screw: cognitive science, quality improvement, and psychotherapy. *Journal of Consulting and Clinical Psychology, 65,* **970-983.**

*Scoggin, F., Bynum, J., Stephens, G., & Calhoun, S. (1990). Efficacy of self-administered treatment programs: Meta-analytic review. *Professional Psychology, 21,* 42-47.

*Scoggin, F., & McElreath, L. (1994). Efficacy of psychosocial treatment for geriatric depression: A quantitative review. *Journal of Consulting and Clinical Psychology, 62,* 68-74.

*Seligman, M. E. P. (1991). *Learned optimism.* New York: Knopf.

*Shibles. W. (1974). *Emotion: The method of philosophical therapy.* Whitewater, WI: Language Press.

*Shihan, V., & Rohrbaugh, M. (1994). Paradoxical intervention. In R. J. Corsini, ed. *Encyclopedia of psychology,* Vol. 3 (pp. 5-8). New York: Wiley.

*Shostrom, E. L. (1976). *Actualizing therapy.* San Diego, CA: Edits.

**Sichel, J., & Ellis, A. (1984). *RET self-help form.* New York: Institute for Rational-Emotive Therapy.

Silverman, M. S., McCarthy, M., & McGovern, T. (1992). A review of outcome studies of rational-emotive therapy from 1982-1989. *Journal of Rational-Emotive and Cognitive-Behavior Therapy, 10*(3), 111-186.

**Simon, J. L. (1993). *Good mood.* LaSalle, IL: Open Court.

*Smith, M. L., & Glass, G. V. (1977). Meta-analysis of psychotherapy outcome studies. *American Psychologist, 32,* 752-760.

*Smith, M. L., Glass, G. V., & Miller, T. I. (1980). *The benefits of psychotherapy.* Baltimore: Johns Hopkins University Press.

*Sookman, D., Pinard, G., & Beauchemin, N. (1994). Multidimensional schematic restructuring treatment for obsessions: Theory and practice. *Journal of Cognitive Psychotherapy, 8,* 175-207.

**Spillane, R. (1985). *Achieving peak performance: A psychology of success in the organization.* Sydney, Australia: Harper & Row.

*Spivack, G., Platt, J., & Shure, M. (1976). *The problem-solving approach to adjustment.* San Francisco: Jossey-Bass.

*Spivack, G., & Shure, M. (1974). *Social adjustment in young children.* San Francisco: Jossey-Bass.

*Stanton, H. (1977). The utilization of suggestions derived from rational-emotive therapy. *International Journal of Clinical and Experimental Hypnosis, 25,* 18-26.

*Stanton, H. E. (1989). Hypnosis and rational-emotive therapy — A de-stressing combination. *International Journal of Clinical and Experimental Hypnosis, 37,* 95-99.

*Starker, S. (1988a). Do-it-yourself therapy. *Psychotherapy, 25,* 142-146.

*Starker, S. (1988b). Psychologists and self-help books. *American Journal of Psychotherapy, 43,* 448-455.

*Stroud, W. L., Jr. (1994). A cognitive-behavioral view of agency and freedom. *American Psychologist, 44,* 142-143.

Sullivan, H. S. (1953). *The interpersonal theory of psychiatry.* New York: Norton.

*Thorne, F. C. (1950). *Principles of personality counseling.* Brandon, VT: Journal of Clinical Psychology Press.

Tillich, P. (1953). *The courage to be.* New York: Oxford.

*Tosi, D. J., Fuller, J., & Gwynne, P. (1980, June). The treatment of hyperactivity and learning disabilities through RSDH. Paper presented at the Third Annual Conference in Rational Emotive Therapy, New York.

*Tosi, D. J., Judha, S. M., & Murphy, M. M. (1989). The effects of a cognitive experiential therapy utilizing hypnosis, cognitive restructuring, and developmental staging on psychological factors associated with duodenal ulcer. *Journal of Cognitive Psychotherapy, 3,* 273-290.

*Tosi, D., & Marzella, J. N. (1977). The treatment of guilt through rational stage directed therapy. In J. L. Wolfe & E. Brand, eds. *Twenty years of rational therapy* (pp. 234-240). New York: Institute for Rational-Emotive Therapy.

*Tosi, D., & Reardon, J. P. (1976). The treatment of guilt through rational stage directed therapy. *Rational Living, 11*(1), 8-11.

*Tosi, D. J., Rudy, D. R., Lewis, J., & Murphy, M. A. (1992). The psychobiological effects of cognitive experiential therapy, hypnosis, cognitive restructuring, and attention placebo control in the treatment of essential hypertension. *Psychotherapy, 29,* 274-284.

**Trimpey, J. (1989). *Rational recovery from alcoholism: The small book.* New York: Delacorte.

*Trimpey, J. (1993). Step zero: Addiction voice recognition technique. *Journal of Rational Recovery, 6*(1), 5-7.

*Trimpey, J. (1994). AVRT in a nutshell.

*Trimpey, J., & Trimpey, L. (1990). *Rational recovery from fatness.* Lotus, CA: Lotus Press.

Tyler, F. B., Brome, D. B., & Williams, J. E. (1991). *Ethnic validity, ecology and psychotherapy.* New York: Plenum.

**Velten, E., speaker. (1987). *How to be unhappy at work.* Cassette recording. New York: Institute for Rational-Emotive Therapy.

*Vernon, A. (1989). *Thinking, feeling, behaving: An emotional education curriculum for children.* Champaign, IL: Research Press.

*Wachtel, P. L. (1977). *Psychoanalysis and behavior therapy: Toward an integration.* New York: Basic Books.

*Wachtel, P. L. (1994). Cyclical processes in personality and psychopathology. *Journal of Abnormal Psychology, 103,* 51-54.

*Walen, S., DiGiuseppe, R., & Dryden, W. (1992). *A practitioner's guide to rational-emotive therapy.* New York: Oxford University Press.